WORKS TRAMS OF THE BRITISH ISLES

A SURVEY OF TRAMWAY ENGINEERS' VEHICLES

WORKS TRAMS OF
THE BRITISH ISLES

A SURVEY OF TRAMWAY ENGINEERS' VEHICLES

PETER WALLER

PEN & SWORD
TRANSPORT

AN IMPRINT OF PEN & SWORD BOOKS LTD.
YORKSHIRE - PHILADELPHIA

First published in Great Britain in 2019 by
Pen and Sword Transport
An imprint of
Pen & Sword Books Ltd
Yorkshire - Philadelphia

ISBN 978 1 47386 223 4

A CIP catalogue record for this book is available from the British Library.

Typeset by Aura Technology and Software Services, India
Printed and bound in India by Replika Press Pvt. Ltd.

Pen & Sword Books Ltd incorporates the Imprints of Pen & Sword Books Archaeology, Atlas, Aviation,
Battleground, Discovery, Family History, History, Maritime, Military, Naval, Politics, Railways, Select,
Transport, True Crime, Fiction, Frontline Books, Leo Cooper, Praetorian Press, Seaforth Publishing,
Wharncliffe and White Owl.

For a complete list of Pen & Sword titles please contact

PEN & SWORD BOOKS LIMITED
47 Church Street, Barnsley, South Yorkshire, S70 2AS, England
E-mail: enquiries@pen-and-sword.co.uk
Website: www.pen-and-sword.co.uk

or

PEN AND SWORD BOOKS
1950 Lawrence Rd, Havertown, PA 19083, USA
E-mail: Uspen-and-sword@casematepublishers.com
Website: www.penandswordbooks.com

CONTENTS

ACKNOWLEDGEMENTS

The majority of the images in this book have been drawn from the collections held by the Online Transport Archive; these include the following: the late Robin Barratt, Barry Cross, the late C. Carter, the late Les Collings, the late Ian Crombie, the late Gerald Druce, the late Dr E.R. Clarke, the late W.S. Eades, the late Marcus Eavis, the late George Fairley, the late Philip Hanson, the late W.G.S. Hyde, the late D.W.K. Jones (postcard collection), the late R.W.A. Jones, the late J. Joyce, the late F.N.T. Lloyd-Jones, LRTA (London Area), the late Harry Luff, the late John McCann, John Meredith, the late Geoffrey Morant, Hamish Stevenson, the late Ronnie Stephens, the late Ian Stewart, the late Phil Tatt, the late Julian Thompson, the late F.E.J. Ward, the late Peter N. Williams, the late Reg Wilson, Ian L. Wright and the late W.J. Wyse. The National Tramway Museum houses the negatives of the late W.A. Camwell, the late Maurice O'Connor and the late R.B. Parr. As with my earlier books, I'd like to express my sincere thanks to Martin Jenkins. I would also like to express my gratitude to Barry Cross for his comments and ideas.

ABBREVIATIONS

ARP	Air Raid Precautions
BEC	British Electric Car Co Ltd, Trafford Park, Manchester
BET	British Electric Traction
CIÉ	Córas Iompair Éireann
DUT	Dublin United Tramways
ERTCW	Electric Railway & Tramway Carriage Works
LCC	London County Council
LMS	London, Midland & Scottish Railway
LPTB	London Passenger Transport Board
L&CBER	Llandudno & Colwyn Bay Electric Railway
LUT	London United Tramways
M&G	Mountain and Gibson
MET	Metropolitan Electric Tramways
NTM	National Tramway Museum
UEC	United Electric Car Co Ltd

INTRODUCTION

Often little known and generally unfamiliar to the passengers that used tramways, works trams were an essential facet of the efficient operation of any system – large or small – and this book is a primarily pictorial overview of the great variety of works trams that served the first generation of tramways in the British Isles.

Although construction of most tramways was left to the contractor employed on the work, once this was completed, the responsibility for the maintenance and safe operation of the system fell on the operator. This applied equally to those tramways that were operated by the local authorities as well as those leased to commercial operators, such as the myriad subsidiaries of British Electric Traction. The larger the operator, the greater and more varied the fleet of works cars employed; specialist vehicles were constructed for specific duties. Smaller operators, however, did not have this luxury, relying instead on one or two dedicated works cars or, more often, a passenger car temporarily assigned to that work.

The range of work undertaken was impressive. This included the regular relaying of tram track and overhead maintenance and, courtesy of the provision of the Tramways Act of 1870, the responsibility of maintaining the road surface between the tramway tracks and to a distance of 18in either side of the outer running rail. As more systems invested in segregated reservations so it became necessary to invest in equipment capable of operating away from the public highway such as rail-borne tower wagons. There was an additional aspect to the story of many tramways; a number also saw the potential for additional revenue from freight and parcels traffic, and dedicated vehicles were again constructed for this type of work. Tramways like Glasgow and Huddersfield selected the 4ft 7¾in gauge rather than standard gauge as it facilitated the operation of conventional railway wagons over their systems; the most famous example of this work was probably the electric locomotive that plied its trade for the Fairfield Shipbuilding & Engineering Co in Govan that outlasted the tramway and was converted to operate using the replacement trolleybus overhead.

Aside from the passenger cars that were occasionally pressed into service as works cars and those trams purpose-built for the purpose, a significant number of ex-passenger cars were converted for works duties once their earlier career was completed. As late as the early 1950s, Liverpool Corporation was still converting redundant passenger cars into snow ploughs, for example, and the now restored LCC No 106 at the National Tramway Museum was to spend the latter part of its career as a snow plough (No 022). A number of works cars – such as Cardiff No 131 – survive in preservation; a number now undertake similar duties in preservation as they did during their working lives at places like Crich and Heaton Park.

Most of the duties undertaken by works cars are relatively self-explanatory; snow ploughs and salt wagons, for example, were employed largely to deal with wintry conditions whilst sett cars were utilised for the movement of road setts to create decent road surfaces, pursuant to the 1870 Act, once the track had been laid. In order to ensure good electric connections, welding equipment was used to help bond the rail joints. Some operators employed specialist vehicles with welding equipment included, whilst for others, welding kit was moved from site to site using general works cars. Railgrinders and scrubbers were designed to improve the running quality of the track. Carborundum blocks were employed to rub along the rail surface in order to eradicate track corrugations; this required considerable pressure and so railgrinding cars were often combined with water carriers. The latter were a feature of tramways from the earliest days. In an era before most road surfaces were made up, dust was a major problem. This could be disturbed by non-tramway traffic and would settle in the grooved tramway track. This might cause the trams' trucks or bogies to ride less well and thus make less of an electric contact – an essential feature of electric tramcar operation was the return connection provided by the track without which the entire tram might become 'live' and thus potentially result in passengers or crew being given a significant electric shock – and so elimination of this dust was essential. Water cars, fitted with large tanks, were thus often the only dedicated works car acquired by an operator. Used primarily in the summer months to spray water, the use of this type of tram diminished during the course of the twentieth century as road surfaces generally improved to cater for the increased traffic in the years after the First World War.

Whilst many of the vehicles used in tramway construction and maintenance were rail-borne, many operators also employed road vehicles. In the earliest days, these were often horse-drawn but the development of steam wagons and the internal combustion engine saw an increasing number of motorised vehicles – most notably tower wagons – from the early twentieth century.

The scale of some of the civil engineering work undertaken for tramway construction was massive. This view of the Clock Tower in Leicester was taken in 1904 and shows the complex network of track required at this important intersection being installed. In the early days much of the equipment utilised was relatively primitive and the work was labour intensive; over the next half century, specialist equipment was developed that aided both tramway construction and maintenance. (J. Joyce Collection/Online Transport Archive)

Many small tramway operators did not acquire any purpose-built works cars, relying on using passenger cars for such work. One such operator was Barking UDC in east London, where No 4 – one of seven open-top trams supplied for the system's opening in 1903 on Peckham Cantilever four-wheel trucks – was employed for a number of years for permanent way and breakdown duties. The car here is seen in original condition with reversed stairs; it was partially rebuilt in 1922 when direct stairs were fitted. It was scrapped four years later. (Barry Cross Collection/Online Transport Archive)

Construction and maintenance of the tramway was labour intensive, particularly as the operator was responsible for the road surface to either side of the running lines as well. This view taken in Leeds shows one of the corporation's tippler wagons in use; nine similar vehicles were supplied before the First World War – the first two in 1906 and the remainder in 1910. They were all fitted with Peckham Cantilever four-wheel trucks. A further nine were acquired between 1917 and 1922. (D.W.K. Jones Collection/Online Transport Archive)

On 12 February 1950, a week before the last trams in the city operated, Cardiff Corporation No 66 heads outbound along Whitchurch Road whilst work is in progress utilising two of the corporation's tower wagons on modifying the overhead to permit trolleybus operation on the route. Closest to the camera is converted pre-war Leyland Titan KG8904; like a number of other operators, Cardiff made use of redundant but modified buses as part of its service fleet. (Ian L. Wright/Online Transport Archive)

The complexity of major trackwork is demonstrated all too clearly in this view of laying new conduit track in London. Specialist equipment was required for much of the work but it was also labour intensive. The conduit track itself added to the complexity, with vehicles dedicated to the specific needs of maintenance. (Julian Thompson/Online Transport Archive)

It's 29 December 1951 and London's trams have less than eight months before final abandonment, but work on repairing the system goes on along Dulwich Road. Note the poles attached to the roadside equipment; these meant that the equipment could be fed with electricity from the overhead whilst not disrupting the services along the route. (Julian Thompson/Online Transport Archive)

Work is in hand on the track at Brixton Hill as a route 18 tram awaits clearance to head south towards Croydon and Purley. Even in the late 1940s, work on track relaying was labour intensive, particularly in terms of laying the setts, but there was also some line-side equipment, such as welding gear and tar boilers, that were essential for the completion of the work. (J. Joyce Collection/Online Transport Archive)

The last major trackwork undertaken in London occurred during 1950 in order to create a one-way loop at the south end of Westminster Bridge adjacent to County Hall in connection with the following year's Festival of Britain. This view records the work in progress as a 'Feltham' passes in the background on a route 16 service. The new trackwork opened in two stages during 1950, but was destined to have only a relatively short life. (F.E.J. Ward/Online Transport Archive)

A further view of the creation of the new one-way loop – on 1 August 1950 – sees the tramway track under construction in Lambeth Palace Road with Westminster Bridge Road in the background. (John Meredith/ Online Transport Archive)

Although many tramways employed dedicated rail grinders for smaller jobs – such as this trackwork being undertaken in London – hand-held grinders were often more practical. (F.E.J. Ward/Online Transport Archive)

All eyes – even that of the pedestrian on the right – seem to be on the photographer in Sheffield as a track gang undertakes work. Note the man on the right pouring tar to help secure and waterproof the setts. (Phil Tatt/Online Transport Archive)

A Belfast 'McCreary' car has suffered damage to its trolleypole on 15 June 1953. Whilst the crew wait for the offending item to be repaired, the maintenance crew undertake the work from the platform of AEC tower wagon T.W.53 (MZ2322). (Julian Thompson/Online Transport Archive)

Recorded in Swinegate depot are three of Leeds Corporation's extensive fleet of works car. On the extreme left is No 1; this was a rail derrick that was converted from No 80A (originally Brush-built No 80 of 1902 on a Peckham Cantilever four-wheel truck) in about January 1935; this was to survive in service until July 1953. In the centre is railgrinder No2; this was built by the corporation itself in 1905 on an old steam car locomotive truck. Effectively replaced in 1939, it was refurbished in October 1952 and re-entered service – albeit not without problems – in February 1955. It was finally scrapped in May 1955. On the right – and unrenumbered – is No 377, which was used with sister car No 378 as a towing car from 1952 and 1951 respectively; note the chain attached to the vestibule end. Nos 377 and 378 were corporation-built cars on Peckham P22 four-wheel trucks that dated originally to 1924. (Barry Cross Collection/Online Transport Archive)

It's 24 March 1956 and the last operational day of the Llandudno & Colwyn Bay Electric Railway but running repairs are still required. Here, the company's tower wagon is seen at Brompton Bridge as the track gang undertake emergency repairs. Following the line's closure, the tower wagon's final duties would be to assist in the removal of the overhead as the line was dismantled. (F.E.J. Ward/Online Transport Archive)

For many of the works vehicles employed by the tramway operators, the final duties – usually long after the last passenger cars had been consigned to the scrapyards – involved dismantling the equipment that they had once helped to maintain. This view of Edinburgh sees two of the corporation's tower wagons – FSF784 and AWS632 – employed in the sad work of removing the overhead. (George Fairley Collection/Online Transport Archive)

The trolleypole from one of Blackpool Corporation's railcoaches requires the attention of the maintenance gang. The tower wagon is No 238 (CFV295) which was manufactured by Karrier and was new in 1948; it was to see some 17 years' service before withdrawal in 1965. (J. Joyce Collection/Online Transport Archive)

Most tramway operators employed road vehicles alongside their works trams. This Thornycroft – UH9004 – was employed by Cardiff Corporation as a lorry for the movement of traction columns; as the city's trolleybus system outlasted the trams, the vehicle survived the closure of the tramway system in March 1950 and is seen in the corporation's Newport road depot on 20 July 1954. (Ian L. Wright/Online Transport Archive)

GENERAL WORKS CARS

In October 1902, Chatham & District Light Railways Co No 19 – one of a batch of 25 trams supplied by G.F. Milnes & Co that year on Brill 21E four-wheel trucks – was seriously damaged in an accident; not repaired, the truck and electrical equipment were, however, used the following year in the construction of the fleet's only dedicated works car. Converted in the company's own workshops at Luton Road, the new vehicle – unnumbered when new but given the number 19 when modified in 1928 – was fitted with an M&G-built water tank. The car is pictured here in original – and unnumbered – condition in 1921. It was to survive until the system's demise in late 1930 and was subsequently scrapped. (D.W.K. Jones Collection/Online Transport Archive)

Believed to have been constructed at Dundalk in 1903, Hill of Howth No 11 was a goods car initially and afterwards it became the line's works car. When built, it lacked dedicated running gear, being fitted with such equipment as and when required from one of the passenger fleet. No 1 was eventually fitted with Brill 22E maximum traction bogies. As with the passenger fleet, No 11 survived until the line's closure and was acquired for preservation locally. Unfortunately, suffering from vandalism, the remains of No 11 were eventually scrapped.
(Barry Cross Collection/Online Transport Archive)

Brighton Corporation's sole dedicated works car was this car, which was numbered 1 eventually. Its origins are obscure; one source suggests that it was a converted ex-Brighton & Shoreham Tramway horse car but it is generally regarded as having been constructed at Lewes Road works in 1909 and was originally an unnumbered snow broom. At a later date, it was converted into a works car, combining rail grinding, thermit welding and general breakdown duties. With no access to the 'saloon' from either platform, the only entrance was via the side door illustrated – the other side lacked a door but had seven windows rather than the six on the side seen here. Fitted with a Brill 21E four-wheel truck, the car was to survive until towards the end of the Brighton system but was scrapped before the final trams operated in 1939. (Barry Cross Collection/Online Transport Archive)

In 1911, Belfast Corporation acquired a four-wheel stores van; its exact provenance is uncertain, but it was probably constructed in the corporation's Sandy Row workshops. No 8 was fitted with a Brill 21E 5ft 6in wheelbase truck salvaged from one of the electrified horse trams. No 8 was to survive in service until the system's closure in 1954. (Barry Cross Collection/Online Transport Archive)

In 1915, Plymouth Corporation took over the operation of the Devonport & District Tramways Co; at the same time it acquired some 27 trams from the latter. Of these, 15 entered service immediately but the remaining 12 were held in store until 1918 and only then, following re-equipment, were introduced. Three of the latter twelve – Nos 75, 79 and 83 – were converted to works duties. All three had originally been part of the original batch of 20 open-top trams supplied to the Devonport company by the Philadelphia-based J.G. Brill Co on the same manufacturer's 21E four-wheel trucks. No 79, as illustrated here, had received an extended canopy in Plymouth prior to being converted into a single-deck breakdown car. (W.A. Camwell/National Tramway Museum)

Wigan Corporation was unusual in operating both 3ft 6in and 4ft 8½in gauge electric trams. In 1923, two years before the final demise of the narrow gauge system, one of the 3ft 6in trams was converted into a standard gauge works car. Unnumbered after conversion, the tram pictured here was rebuilt from one of a batch of twelve open-top double-deck cars, Nos 13-24, supplied originally by ERTCW on Brill 21E trucks in 1901. All received top covers between 1903 and 1906 and, with the exception of No 24 (which reverted to open top in 1919), replacement top covers between 1913 and 1917. A number were subsequently cut down to single-deck. The final standard gauge Wigan trams operated on 30 September 1931. (Barry Cross Collection/Online Transport Archive)

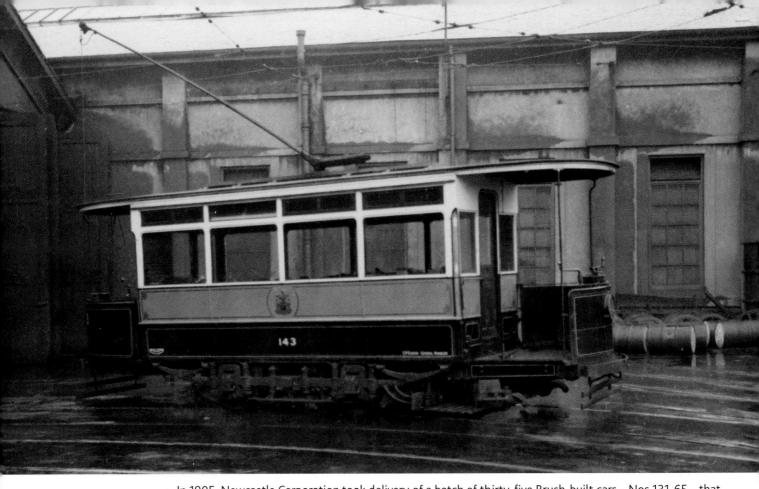

In 1905, Newcastle Corporation took delivery of a batch of thirty-five Brush-built cars – Nos 131-65 – that were designated Class D. These were open-top vehicles fitted with Brill 21E four-wheel trucks. All of the type had been withdrawn by 1939 but seven were converted into works cars during that decade. Six – Nos 133/38/40/41/42/44 – were primarily used as snow ploughs with two – Nos 138 and 144 – being scrapped before the start of the war. The seventh – No 143 seen here as converted – was utilised as a breakdown car. No 143 was one of six that were converted during the First World War to act as coupled units; two trams were permanently coupled, losing one trolleypole and the innermost controllers but gaining air brakes. They operated in this guise until 1925. (R. Elliott)

Prior to the acquisition of No DE320224 (see page 25), the Grimsby & Immingham operated No 5 as a dedicated works car. This was one of a quartet of cars – Nos 5-8 – that were built by Brush in 1911 that were shorter than Nos 1-4. Nos 5-8 were designed for the possible operation beyond the Corporation Bridge terminus over the track owned by Grimsby Corporation. All four were withdrawn from service in 1931, when No 5 was converted into a works car. It is seen here towards the end of its life outside Pyewipe depot now in the ownership of British Railways. (R.B. Parr/National Tramway Museum)

Alongside the ten open-top double-deck trams acquired by the Llandudno & Colwyn Bay Electric Railway from Bournemouth Corporation in 1936, the company also acquired an eleventh car – No 23 – which was to become the system's works car. No 23 had originally been one of the first quartet of open-top trams, Nos 1-4, supplied by G.F. Milnes & Co to the Poole & District Tramways Co Ltd in 1901. Poole & District was purchased by Poole Corporation on 15 June 1903 and operation leased to Bournemouth Corporation two years later; Nos 1-4 were renumbered 55-58 by Bournemouth and, in 1921, No 55 was converted into a single-deck railgrinder. Following the purchase of the two ex-Darwen streamlined trams in 1946, the works car was renumbered 23A in 1947. It was to survive through until the final demise of the L&CBER in 1956. The survival of this tram with four owners is noteworthy. (Phil Tatt/Online Transport Archive)

Following the demise of the Gateshead & District system in 1951, British Railways acquired nineteen single-deck trams in order to supplement and replace some of the existing rolling stock in use on the Grimsby & Immingham line. Of these, seventeen entered passenger service and one was damaged beyond economic repair before entering service; this left one car – ex-Gateshead No 17 (built originally by Brush on Brill 39E bogies) – that was converted to act as a dedicated works car for the line as No DE320224. It is seen here at the line's sole depot – at Pyewipe – alongside the wheeled, but unpowered, tower wagon that was used for the line's overhead repairs. (R. Stephens/Online Transport Archive)

Following withdrawal in July 1953, Blackpool Corporation 'Pullman' No 167 was transferred for works duties. Originally one of a batch of ten – Nos 167-76 – supplied by English Electric on Preston McGuire equal-wheel bogies, No 167 was modified in 1957 when less powerful motors – 35hp rather than 50hp – were installed. It is seen here, in the overall green livery into which it was repainted in 1957, heading south past the Norbreck Hydro. Withdrawn from works duties on 17 March 1962, No 167 was subsequently to be preserved at Crich, where it has been restored to its early 1950s condition – painted green and white – as a passenger car. (W.G.S. Hyde/Online Transport Archive)

MISCELLANEOUS VEHICLES

A handful of systems operated cars designated for the use of the directors. One of these was Dublin, where an unnumbered directors' car was completed at Spa Road works in June 1901; it cost £1,094 when new. Initially fitted with a Peckham truck, this was replaced by one constructed at Spa Road in 1909. Although largely disused from the late 1930s, the car was to survive until the system's closure in 1949 and was sold the following year to Mr H. Porter for £75. Relocated to Dalkey, it was used as a summer house. In 1984 – whilst negotiations were in hand to pass the tram to the Transport Museum Society of Ireland – it suffered serious fire damage. It was transferred to Howth in August 1988 and currently awaits restoration. (Barry Cross Collection/Online Transport Archive)

The interior of the DUT directors' car was lavishly fitted out – as is clear in this view of the lower deck – with accommodation being provided by 12 armchairs. (Barry Cross Collection/Online Transport Archive)

LUT possessed a number of dedicated works cars; No 4 in the fleet – built by the British Electric Car Co in 1903 and fitted with a Brill 21E four-wheel truck – was used as a ticket van. Later renumbered 004, the tram was to pass to the LPTB in 1933 and was to be scrapped later that decade. (Barry Cross Collection/ Online Transport Archive)

Pictured in Coplawhill Works is Glasgow Corporation No 3. This was a mains test car and was converted for the purpose from 'Room & Kitchen' car No 672 in 1908 following withdrawal in August. The twenty-one 'Room & Kitchen' cars, Nos 665-85, were the corporation's first electric trams and entered service during 1897 and 1898. No 3 was fitted with corporation-built equal-wheel bogies and was to survive as a works car until final withdrawal in October 1953. Following a period in store, No 3 was restored between 1959 and 1962 and, as No 672, was to feature in the closure procession in September 1962. The tram is now preserved in the city's Riverside Museum. (Phil Tatt/Online Transport Archive)

Dublin United Trams Nos 21 and 22 are recorded at the PW yard at Donnybrook. No 21 seems to have been originally a horse tram converted for works duties, whilst No 22, which was originally No 5, was a combined locomotive and site office, being referred to as an attendance van. (Barry Cross Collection/Online Transport Archive)

In 1904, Aberdeen Corporation constructed in its King Street workshops a single works car on a Brill 21E four-wheel truck. Unnumbered throughout its career, the tram was initially planned as a general engineering car and stores van but, from 1907, it was designated as an 'Emergency Car' and it is pictured in this guise. Note the unusual bow collector. (W.A. Camwell/National Tramway Museum)

Glasgow Corporation No 21, seen here at the Coplawhill PW yard on 13 June 1962, was a welders' tool van that was new in December 1903. Fitted with a Brill 21E four-wheel truck and originally numbered 1, the tram was similar to half a 'Room & Kitchen' car and it is believed that it was constructed from spare parts from these passenger cars. There is an alternative theory that sees the original No 1 being a converted ex-electrified horse car and this car was constructed in about 1920, but the evidence does not support either theory definitively. What is known is that the tram was fitted with enclosed vestibules in October 1939 and was modernised with a replacement truck and electrical equipment a decade later; following withdrawal when the system closed in September 1962, the tram was preserved and it now forms part of the NTM collection, albeit in an unrestored and inoperable condition. (Les Collings/Online Transport Archive)

Glasgow Corporation No 20, seen here at the junction of Argyle Street and Stockwell Street, was the Mains Department's Tool. This tram had been converted from Paisley District Tramways Co Ltd No 39 – which had originally been built by Brush and delivered in 1904 – which was one of the first Paisley trams to be withdrawn (in 1924) following the corporation's purchase of the company on 1 August 1923. Never renumbered into the corporation fleet, No 39 was converted into a works car in March 1925. Fitted with a Brill 21E truck, No 20, which remained unvestibuled throughout its operational life, was withdrawn for scrap in February 1959. (Phil Tatt/ Online Transport Archive)

In all, Newcastle Corporation employed six sand and salt cars; the first three – Nos 167-69 – were constructed by the corporation in its own workshops on Brill 21E four-wheel trucks in 1904. One of the first three, No 169, is pictured here in Byker depot. This and No 167 were both scrapped before the Second World War. (Barry Cross Collection/ Online Transport Archive)

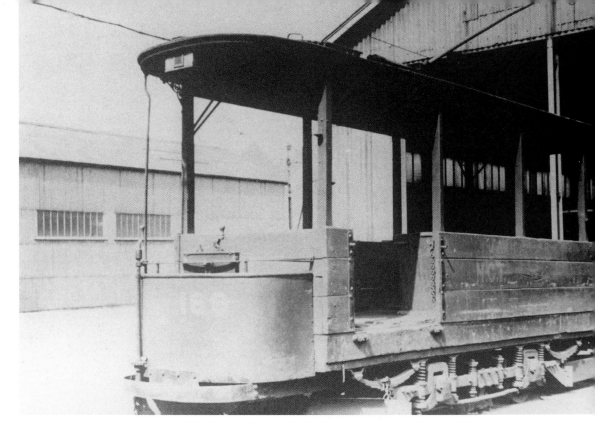

Leeds Corporation possessed two rail-based cranes, both of which were supplied by Joseph Booth & Bros of Rodley in the city. The first was new in 1910, whilst the second followed 12 years later. Each of the cranes had a two-ton capacity and here the older of the two is pictured on the wharf at Sovereign Street. (F.E.J. Ward/ Online Transport Archive)

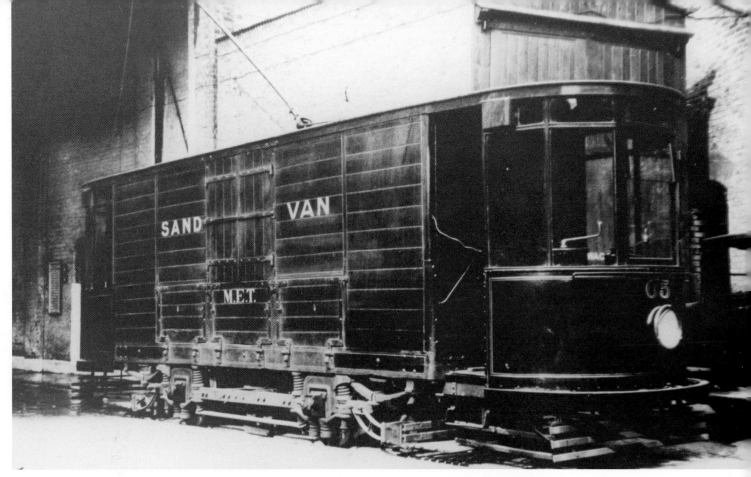

In 1911, the MET's Hendon Works constructed a sand car – No 5 – on a six-wheel Barber-designed truck supplied by the British Radial Axle Cars Ltd to transport dried sand from the sand driers at Wood Green to the MET's four other operational depots. The six-wheel truck was not to survive long, however, being replaced by a more conventional four-wheel Brush-built AA truck in 1913. It was fitted with enclosed platforms in 1926 and it is in this guise that it is recorded here whilst still in MET operation. Surviving to be taken over by the LPTB in July 1933, the vehicle was fitted with a plough to operate over the conduit system. In later years, the car was used to move sand from Poplar and to tow passenger cars to and from Hampstead depot. It was finally to be withdrawn in 1938. (Barry Cross Collection/Online Transport Archive)

In 1913, the LUT acquired a further dedicated works car – No 005 – that was fitted with Brill 22E bogies. Designated as a crane and wheel carrier, the car was to pass to the LPTB in 1933, in whose ownership the car is recorded in this view. No 005 was not to remain in LPTB ownership for long as it was scrapped in 1937. (Barry Cross Collection/ Online Transport Archive)

In 1904, Halifax Corporation acquired two demi-cars – Nos 95 and 96 – that were built by Brush and initially fitted with the same manufacturer's DuPont four-wheel trucks; the latter were eventually replaced by Peckham 9A trucks. The two underwent several rebuilds during their career but, in May 1918, No 96 was converted into a mobile soup kitchen, providing sustenance during a phase of the First World War when there was a severe food shortage in the country as a result of the German U-boat campaign. It is pictured in this guise; after the war, No 96 was cut-down and converted into an unpowered permanent way trailer and was to survive in that form until about 1927. No 95 was used post-war initially as a paying-in car before becoming a works car; it was withdrawn in about 1928. (W.S. Eades Collection/Online Transport Archive)

Dundee Corporation was one of a number of operators that acquired open mineral wagons for the movement of sand. Two wagons – Nos 1 and 2 as illustrated here – were acquired in 1909. (Barry Cross Collection/Online Transport Archive)

The second trio of sand and salt cars operated by Newcastle Corporation, Nos 310-12, were built between 1921 and 1923. Again constructed in the corporation's own workshops on Brill 21E four-wheel trucks, there is evidence that the trio was originally numbered 250-52 when new through until 1925. Two of the three, Nos 310 and 311, are also pictured outside Byker depot. All three survived to operate after the Second World War. (F.N.T. Lloyd-Jones/Online Transport Archive)

During 1924 and 1925, a number of the open-top double-deck trams acquired from the Paisley District Tramways Co Ltd were converted into single-deck for use on the newly opened Duntocher route; an additional car – No 1017 – was converted in January 1925 in a modified form to operate as a driver training car. It was fitted with narrow platform doors and had most of its bulkheads removed to provide better visibility for those assessing the trainee drivers. The tram, which had originally been supplied by BEC as Paisley District No 17, was largely based at Langside depot for the bulk of its career, being used on the section of track along Coplaw Street outside the Samaritan hospital that was not used by regular services, until it was transferred to Coplawhill towards the end of its life. It is seen here on 23 February 1958 outside Coplawhill Works prior to undertaking an enthusiast tour. With the Glasgow system's conversion to bus and trolleybus operation, No 1017 was withdrawn finally in August 1960. Following withdrawal, the body was sold and was to survive until rescued for preservation in a Cambuslang garden. It was transferred to Summerlee in 1991 where full restoration was undertaken, with the tram re-entering service during 1992. (Hamish Stevenson/Online Transport Archive)

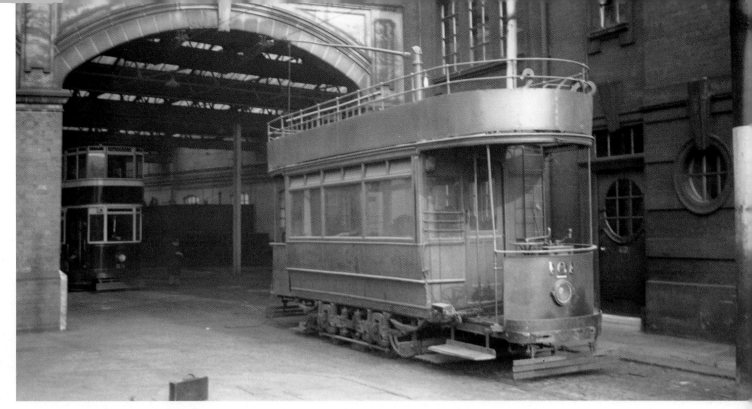

Pictured outside Stockport Corporation's Mersey Square depot is No 101; this had originally been passenger car No 26 – an open-top double-deck car supplied by ERTCW on a Brill 21E truck in 1903 – that was converted to act as a breakdown tram in 1923. It was renumbered 101 six years later. Stockport had three dedicated works cars; in addition to No 101, there was No 100, which was a water car supplied by Dick, Kerr in 1902 (see page 122), and No 102, a salt car, which was converted in 1925 (see page 93). Prior to the construction of No 102, the corporation had employed two ex-horse trams as unpowered trailers for the conveyance of salt. (F.E.J. Ward/Online Transport Archive)

In about 1922, the MET disposed of its second water car – No 2 – and the fleet number was then allocated to a new works car; this was a wheel carrier, which was constructed by the company itself at its Hendon works on M&G 3L bogies. It was destined to survive into LPTB ownership – in whose livery it is pictured here – prior to scrapping in 1937. (D.W.K. Jones Collection/Online Transport Archive)

The MET operated a number of breakdown cars, all of which had been converted from earlier passenger cars. Whilst the majority were reconstructed from ex-MET trams, there was one – the second to bear the number 07 – that was constructed from an ex-Croydon Corporation car – No 43 (new originally in 1906 and built by Brush on an M&G-supplied Brill 21E truck) – that had been acquired from the corporation in June 1927 following withdrawal. Rebuilt by the MET, the new breakdown car replaced an earlier vehicle and was to survive through until final withdrawal in 1936 and was the penultimate ex-MET breakdown car to survive; the last was No 013 of 1931 that was to be withdrawn in 1938. (Barry Cross Collection/Online Transport Archive)

The LCC converted a single ex-Class C car – No 273 of 1904 (one of a batch of 100 cars supplied by Brush on Brill 21E trucks – Nos 202-301 – built that year) – into its sole sand car in about 1930. It is pictured here in the 'Tramatorium' at Penhall Road awaiting its scrapping. (Phil Tatt/ Online Transport Archive)

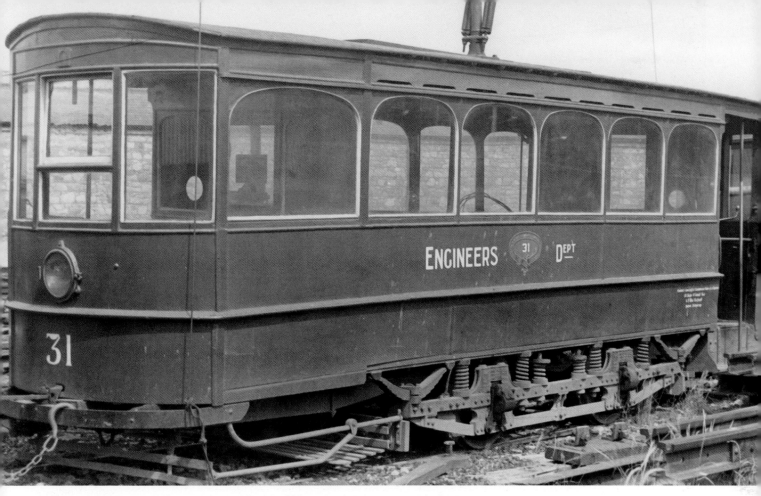

In 1896 and 1898, G.F. Milnes & Co supplied Dublin United Tramways with thirty-seven open-top double-deck cars, all of which were originally fitted with Brill four-wheel trucks. All were withdrawn between 1912 and 1933; one – No 31 – was converted into a works car in 1930. Labelled 'Engineers Dept', the car was to survive through until the closure of the PW yard at Donnybrook in 1947. (Harry Luff collection/Online Transport Archive)

Dublin United Tramways No 99, seen here at Donnybrook, was converted from passenger car No 148; this was one of fifty trams – Nos 121-70 – constructed for the company in the USA and new in 1899. Supplied with a Peckham truck and later fitted with lower deck vestibules, the tram was converted for general works duties in 1932. (Barry Cross Collection/Online Transport Archive)

Aside from a single water car and two salt wagons, Dundee Corporation operated two further works cars – designated 'Repair Wagons' – that were converted from two passenger cars in 1935. Nos 1 and 2 were originally built as part of a batch of six, Nos 55-60, as open balcony double-deck cars by Brush on Brill 21E four-wheel trucks. Nos 56 and 57 were to lose their top decks and be modified for their new role in 1935; both were to survive through to the end of tramcar operation in Dundee in October 1956; one was offered for preservation but, unfortunately, no alternative accommodation could be found and it was scrapped. Here, No 2, ex-No 57, is pictured outside Maryfield depot on 16 August 1950. (Michael H. Waller)

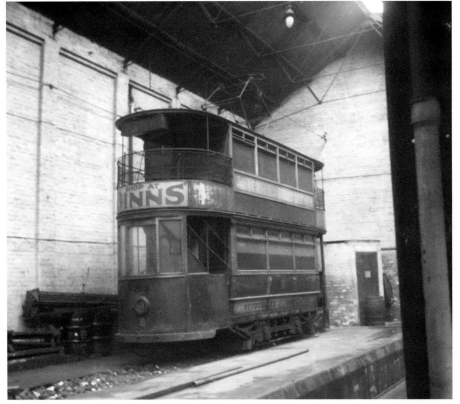

In 1938, Sunderland Corporation converted a redundant passenger car into breakdown car No B. This had originally been No 6, one of the original batch of open-top four-wheel cars supplied to the corporation by ERTCW in 1900. Fitted with Brill 21E trucks, all of the batch were fitted with open-balcony top covers between August 1904 and 1916. Following the purchase of eight fully-enclosed trams from the LPTB in 1938, No 6 was briefly renumbered 46 before its conversion for works duties. No B was to survive through until withdrawal and scrapping in 1951. (J. Joyce/Online Transport Archive)

In May and September 1939, Glasgow Corporation constructed two sand drying cars – Nos 38 and 39 – and the latter of the two is pictured here in Admiral Street. When new, the two cars were fitted with Brill 21E 7ft 0in wheelbase trucks; these were subsequently replaced by similar trucks but with an 8ft 0in wheelbase. Note the special low roof cabs that were a feature of these two vehicles; this was to permit them access through the low entrance into the sand dryer building in Admiral Street. With the contraction of the Glasgow system, No 38 was withdrawn in December 1958 and No 39 in the following September. (Phil Tatt/Online Transport Archive)

Following the conversion of the routes in east London, a batch of six ex-West Ham cars – Nos 325-30 – was stored during the war. After the cessation of hostilities, five – the exception was No 325 that was scrapped at Hampstead – were sent south of the river. However, still fitted with longitudinal seating in the lower deck, none of the quintet was used in public service. Three – Nos 327, 327 and 330 – were used as staff cars to and from Charlton Works and No 327 is pictured here outside the works with the other two in the background. All surviving five were to be scrapped in 1950. (Barry Cross Collection/Online Transport Archive)

Another Sunderland Corporation passenger tram that was to spend its last years as a works car was No 43. This was the last of the fourth batch of trams, Nos 27-50 (supplied to the corporation by the ERTCW on Brill 21E four-wheel trucks in 1901), to survive. Originally No 32 when new, it owed its longevity to the fact that it had been rebuilt as a fully-enclosed car on a Peckham P22 truck in 1925. Renumbered 43 in 1938, following the purchase of eight fully-enclosed trams from Huddersfield Corporation, it was to survive in passenger service until 1951. Finally withdrawn in 1954, it is seen here alongside No 99; the latter was built by English Electric in 1934 and was one of the last wholly new trams acquired by the corporation. (Phil Tatt/Online Transport Archive)

In 1927, Blackpool Corporation constructed six toastrack cars on Preston McGuire bogies; last used in 1939, the six were effectively withdrawn in 1941. In 1951, two of the six – Nos 165 and 166 – were converted to carry television equipment for recording broadcasts of the famous illuminations. Here, No 165 is seen inside Rigby Road depot having had its seating stripped off for use in its television work. (Phil Tatt/Online Transport Archive)

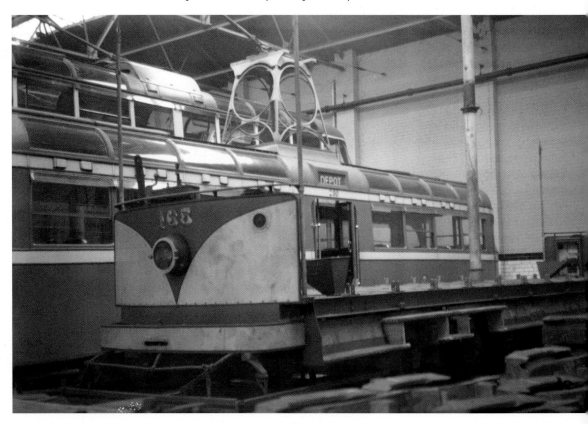

The second of the two trams converted for use by broadcasters was No 166; this, as can be seen in this view of the two in action, retained some of its original seating whilst also providing a platform for a camera and crew. The two were to be renumbered 16 and 17 respectively latterly and were withdrawn in the mid-1960s. Following withdrawal, No 165 was scrapped but No 166 was transferred to the Crich museum in 1972 and restored to its original condition. (W.J. Wyse/LRTA (London Area) Collection/Online Transport Archive)

For the opening of the Manx Electric Railway from Douglas to Groudle Glen in 1893, G.F. Milnes & Co supplied six lightweight trailers on unpowered Milnes bogies. Originally numbered 11-16, they became Nos 23-28 in 1895 and Nos 49-54 during 1903 and 1904. No 52 was used, with its seat and roof removed, as a permanent way flat wagon for a number of years; this arrangement was made permanent in 1954 when its body was scrapped. It is in this condition that the ex-trailer was recorded at Ramsey. It is still available for use on the 3ft 0in gauge line. (F.E.J. Ward/Online Transport Archive)

Following the establishment of a radar station on Snaefell in 1950 by the Air Ministry, the annual removal of the overhead from the upper section of the Snaefell Mountain Railway resulted in the arrival of a Wickham-built trolley; the first of these was No 1. This was Works No 5864 and arrived on the line in 1951. It is pictured here on 19 May 1956 in the RAF blue livery in which it was painted. No 1 survived until 1977 when it was transferred to the MER. It was sold for preservation in the UK in 2007. (M.J. Lea/LRTA (London Area) Collection/Online Transport Archive)

The original Wickham trolley was supplemented in 1957 by a second – No 2 (Works No 7642) – seen here in May 1961 in its original blue livery. Both of these trolleys were repainted yellow and black during the 1960s. No 2 was withdrawn in 1991 and its ultimate fate is unknown. At present, there are two Wickham trolleys still based on the line working for the National Air Traffic Services (successor to the Air Ministry and Civil Aviation Authority); these are No 3 (Works No 10956) that was delivered in 1977 and No 4 (Works No 11730) that arrived fourteen years later (with No 2 being used in part exchange). (W.J. Wyse/LRTA (London Area) Collection/Online Transport Archive)

During the period when London Transport was undertaking the scrapping of trams at Penhall Road, a number of tram bodies were used as offices. One of those so employed was the lower deck of 'E/1' No 1321, which is seen here on 24 September 1950. This new work was to ensure a longer life at the scrapyard than many of its contemporaries; No 1321 was not finally to be disposed of until January 1953, as work on tram dismantling came to an end. (John Meredith/Online Transport Archive)

The last works car conversion undertaken by Glasgow Corporation was in November 1954, when 'Round Dash' No 722, which dated originally from November 1899, was reconstructed into a tool van. The tram, which was fitted with a Brill 21E truck, was to survive until the system's closure and is seen here in the PW yard at Coplawhill on 13 June 1962. (Les Collings/Online Transport Archive)

OVERHEAD LINE AND ELECTRICAL WORK CARS

In an era when motorised vehicles were relatively uncommon, most tramway operators had horse-powered tower wagons to assist with the erection and maintenance of the overhead; this particular example was owned by the Isle of Thanet Tramways & Lighting Co and is pictured outside the company's St Peters depot.
(Barry Cross Collection/Online Transport Archive)

A notable survivor when recorded at Penhall Road on 28 May 1950 was this horse-drawn tower wagon clearly demonstrating its LPTB ownership. For the work in erecting overhead in 1908 and 1909, the LCC acquired a number of tower wagons; these consisted of flat wagons with retractable towers. It was not until 1920 that the LCC acquired its first powered tower wagons but the horse-drawn wagons remained available (five being in service four years later).
(John Meredith/Online Transport Archive)

Not all works vehicles were elegant; this example of a trailer tower wagon was constructed for use by Hull Corporation. It would appear to combine an original horse-drawn vehicle – evinced by the seat at the front – allied to the underframe of a four-wheel wagon.
(Barry Cross Collection/ Online Transport Archive)

In 1901 Halifax Corporation acquired works car No 3; fitted originally with a Brush A four-wheel truck – although this had been replaced by a Peckham cantilever truck from a withdrawn passenger car by the date of this photograph – the vehicle was fitted originally with a wooden tower for overhead line maintenance. The body was constructed by a local joiner – John Hird of Boothtown – and, in its later years, the tram was used primarily for the movement of setts. The final closure of the 3ft 6in gauge Halifax system came on 14 February 1939 and No 3 is seen here towards the end of its life. (W.A. Camwell/National Tramway Museum)

In order the facilitate the laying of cables, Glasgow Corporation's Mains Department employed a dedicated vehicle, No 1, that had been constructed specifically for the role. The tram was constructed by the corporation and fitted with a Brill 21E four-wheel truck. It entered service during 1905 and was to survive through until the end of the system in September 1962; sold for preservation in October 1962, it now forms part of the National Tramway Museum collection. (GCT/Ian Stewart Collection/Online Transport Archive)

P.1078.

This combined tower wagon and mobile crane was constructed for Birmingham Corporation by the Warwick-based Eagle Engineering Co Ltd. (Dr E.R. Clarke Collection/Online Transport Archive)

In 1911, the Tyneside Tramways & Tramroads Co supplemented its fleet of 26 passenger cars through the purchase – probably from UEC – of a single works car, No 27, that was designed as a tower wagon. Fitted with a Brill 21E four-wheel truck, the rail-based wagon would have been particularly useful for the company as its route from Walker to Gosforth included a significant section of track on a private right of way through Benton. The fleet number was reused by the company in 1920, when four open-top double-deck passenger cars – Nos 27-30 – were added to the fleet; these were the last additions and the company ceased tram operation a decade later. (Barry Cross Collection/Online Transport Archive)

The Grimsby & Immingham operated an unpowered trailer tower wagon – seen here at Pyewipe depot –
that was purchased for preservation by J.H. Price following the line's closure in 1961 and transferred to Crich.
(J. Joyce/Online Transport Archive)

The original passenger trams supplied to Blackpool were powered by the conduit system; never wholly successful, the line was converted to overhead operation in 1899. Of the trams supplied for the conduit line, 18 in all, 16 were to be fitted with trolleypoles for operation after conversion. Of these, four – Nos 3-6 – had been built by the Lancaster Railway Carriage & Wagon Co Ltd in 1885 on trunnion trucks; these were replaced by four-wheel trucks supplied by the Wolverhampton-based Electric Construction Co Ltd in 1896. Of this quartet, No 4 – renumbered 1 – was to be converted into an overhead car in 1912. Surviving in this guise for almost 50 years, the tram was one of a number of historic trams to be restored in 1960 in order to mark the 75th anniversary of the opening of the Blackpool system. Subsequently preserved, the tram now forms part of the collection held by the National Tramway Museum. It is seen here, as No 1, in Bispham depot. (F.E.J. Ward/Online Transport Archive)

Dublin United Tramways tower wagon No 75 had originally been constructed for use by the Dublin & Lucan; following that company's cessation of operation in 1925 and the conversion of the bulk of its route from 3ft 6in to 5ft 3in to permit the reintroduction of services three years later, the tower wagon was fitted with a 5ft 3in gauge truck for use on the line. (Barry Cross Collection/Online Transport Archive)

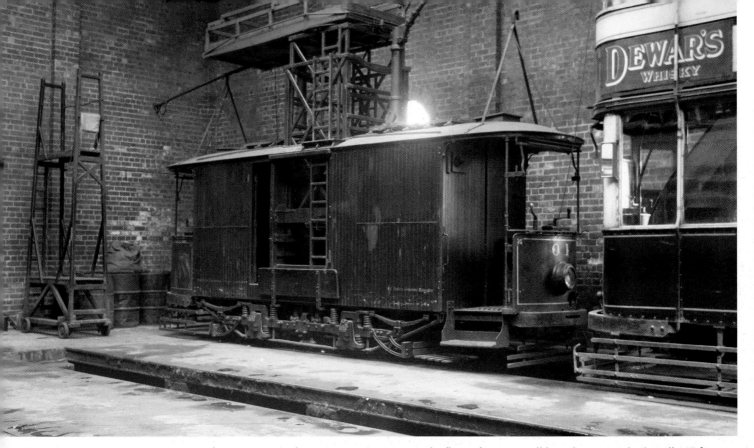

By early 1907, Birmingham Corporation operated a fleet of six vans, all based on M&G-built Brill 21E four-wheel trucks; in 1904, one of these – No 4 – was transferred to the supply of dried sand. A decade later, in August 1924, the tram was modified to act as a tower wagon for work on the reserved track sections of the system. As modified, the tram was allocated to Miller Street depot and renumbered 01. Over the years, the car underwent further modification; these included: in April 1929, the installation of twin trolleypoles; in November 1938 the addition of collapsible rails to the platform; and, finally, a replacement roof was fitted at Witton depot in 1947. As No 01, the overhead wagon was to survive in service until March 1952; it was subsequently scrapped. (F.E.J. Ward/Online Transport Archive)

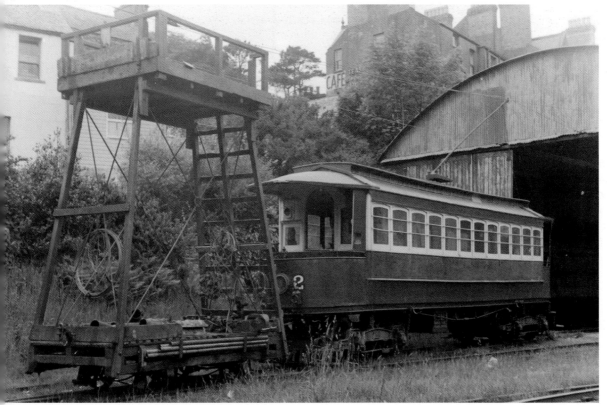

In April 1930, the Manx Electric Railway suffered a major fire at its depot at Laxey. A number of passenger cars were destroyed, as were the three rail-based tower wagons that the line used for overhead maintenance. As a result, the following year, two new tower wagons – Nos 1 and 3 – were constructed by the railway at Derby Castle. One of the two is pictured here outside Derby Castle depot with motor car No 2. Both of the 1931-built tower wagons were withdrawn in 1978 and scrapped the following year. (W.J. Wyse/ LRTA (London Area) Collection/ Online Transport Archive)

With a number of segregated sections of track either completed or planned, Leeds Corporation constructed a new rail-based tower wagon – No 2 – that entered service in December 1931 based around the Peckham Cantilever four-wheel truck of withdrawn No 110A. This was one of a batch of 50 trams supplied by Brush in 1902 and No 110, as the tram was originally numbered, was one of those that had its truck modified to permit operation on the through service to Bradford that required a change of gauge – from 4ft 8½in to 4ft 0in – in Stanningley. Unusually, when new, No 2 was fitted with both a trolleypole and a bow collector; the trolleypole was replaced by a second bow collector in 1938. In late 1953, the old Peckham truck was replaced by the truck from tower wagon No 1 – see page 56 – and for the last years of its operational life in Leeds, No 2 was renumbered 1 from its re-entry to service in December 1953. With the reduction in the Leeds system, the use of the tram declined, although it was to survive until the final closure of the system in November 1959. Preserved on withdrawal, initially on the Middleton Railway, No 2 was transferred to Crich in 1969 and it remains part of the National Tramway Museum collection. The tram is pictured here on Sovereign Street on 8 October 1950. (R.B. Parr/NTM)

Blackpool Corporation No 4 was converted into an engineering car with tower in 1934. This had originally been No 31 from a batch of fifteen, Nos 27-41, known as 'Marton Box' cars that had been supplied by the Midland Railway Carriage & Wagon Co in 1901. Supplied with the same manufacturer's four-wheel trucks, fourteen were to receive replacements between 1906 and 1931. No 31 was one of five rebuilt as bogie cars between 1917 and 1919, receiving Hurst Nelson bogies at the time; an open balcony top cover was added in 1928. The enclosed lower-deck vestibules were added when the car was converted in 1934. In 1972, No 4 was renumbered 754 and was to remain in service until April 1983. Preserved on withdrawal, the tram was restored back to the open-top condition in which it operated up until 1928 as No 31 by the museum at Beamish. Based at Beamish since mid-1984, the tram spent a period during 1998/99 back in Blackpool as the system celebrated the centenary of the route to Fleetwood. (Phil Tatt/Online Transport Archive)

Pictured outside Torre Road depot is Leeds Corporation engineer's breakdown car No 1, which was converted from a redundant passenger car – No 80A – in 1935. This car – new as No 80 in 1902 – had originally been one of fifty open-top trams supplied by Brush and fitted with Peckham Cantilever four-wheel trucks. No 80 was to receive a top cover in 1904 but never received enclosed lower-deck vestibules. Its conversion into a works car included the installation of a derrick for overhead line work. No 1 was withdrawn in July 1953 and scrapped in April 1954. (Geoffrey Morant Collection/Online Transport Archive)

Blackpool Corporation No 753 is seen at Bispham in 1974. The car had originally been 'Standard' No 143 and had been constructed by the corporation at Rigby Road on Hurst Nelson bogies in 1926. Constructed with open balconies and open vestibules, the car received enclosed lower-deck vestibules in December 1929 and was converted to fully enclosed in February 1932. By the late 1950s, the majority of the 'Standard' class had been withdrawn – only a handful survived into the 1960s – and No 143 was taken out of service in 1957. The car was to emerge in July 1958 having been converted into a works car. It was fitted with a diesel generator; an 8.6 litre engine sourced from a redundant Leyland TD5, to enable it to operate when the power was switched off; and an inspection platform. In this guise, it was to operate through until 1990 when, after a fire, it was withdrawn. Although it was expected to be scrapped, the tram was secured for preservation by the Lancashire Transport Trust. It returned to Blackpool in 2013 and is undergoing restoration to original – i.e. open balcony and open vestibule – condition; at the time of writing, it is expected that this car will re-enter service for the first time since 1990 during 2019. (Gerald Druce/Online Transport Archive)

The most recent overhead line car supplied to Blackpool Corporation is No 754; this was built by East Lancashire Coachbuilders of Blackburn (a company that had recently supplied the 'Centenary' class of single-deck trams to the corporation), and was new in 1992. Seen here in Rigby Road depot on 30 July 1993, the tram is fitted with an inspection platform as well as a diesel generator for use when the power is switched off. (R.L. Wilson/Online Transport Archive)

RAILGRINDERS AND SCRUBBERS

The small 3ft 6in gauge system owned by Lowestoft Corporation operated 15 double-deck open-top and four single-deck passenger trams. In addition, it possessed a single – unnumbered – works car that was supplied in 1903 by Brecknell, Munro & Rogers on Brush-built reversed maximum traction bogies. Designed for sweeping and water spraying, the brushes used for sweeping the track can be clearly seen. The Lowestoft system was converted to bus operation in May 1931. (Barry Cross Collection/Online Transport Archive)

In 1904, the LCC constructed four combined water cars and rail grinders on M&G four-wheel trucks; Nos 01-04 were designated as Class H and all four were to pass to the LPTB in July 1933. As road surfaces improved, so the necessity of using water to damp down the dust was reduced, with the cars latterly being used exclusively on rail grinding work, with the water being required to act as a lubricant. No 2 is pictured here at Norwood depot on 5 May 1951; this was the penultimate car of the quartet to survive as it was not to be scrapped at Penhall Road until April 1952. The last of all, No 3, was to succumb two months later. (Peter N. Williams/Online Transport Archive)

The relatively small – 7½-mile long – Reading Corporation system employed a single dedicated works car alongside its fleet of 36 passenger cars; this was a combined railgrinder and water car – No 37 – that was supplied by ERTCW on a Brill 21E four-wheel truck in 1904. This side view, taken on 28 July 1921, shows to good effect the vehicle's construction. The tram was nicknamed by staff the 'watercart' and could be fitted with a snow plough when required. The corporation also owned a small open wagon and a tar boiler; these were towed by No 37 as and when necessary. (D.W.K. Jones Collection/Online Transport Archive)

Manchester Corporation possessed two railgrinders, Nos 1 and 2, both of which were constructed on a Brill 21E four-wheel truck. No 1, illustrated here, was the slightly smaller of the two; it was withdrawn by 1940, but the second was to survive through to the system's closure in 1949. Both were controlled by a single centrally-placed conventional controller and brake as can be seen through the doorway. (W.S. Eades Collection/ Online Transport Archive)

One of the strangest looking vehicles ever to have operated on a British tramway and appearing as something that a mad scientist might have dreamt up in an alcohol induced stupor, this piece of specialised equipment was a rail grinder produced in Plymouth Corporation's Compton depot in 1915; it was to survive in service until 1935. (Barry Cross Collection/Online Transport Archive)

Alongside its two water cars, Hull Corporation possessed a rail grinder. This was built by the corporation itself in 1916 on a Brill 21E four-wheel truck in 1916. It is pictured here on 6 May 1936. (Barry Cross Collection/ Online Transport Archive)

In 1920, Bradford Corporation constructed a new railgrinder – No 11 – which is pictured here on the approach track within Thornbury depot along with two of the passenger cars cut down to single-deck for use as works cars. No 11 incorporated the trolleypole used originally by an electric locomotive that had operated at the nearby Phoenix Works of the Phoenix Dynamo Manufacturing Co (part of English Electric after 1918) combined with the cabs reused from two of Bradford's pioneering trolleybuses. No 11 was to survive in service until withdrawal in June 1949. The track on which No 11 is standing was used briefly, following the restoration of Bradford No 104, for the operation of the tram, using the trolleybus overhead between 1958 and 1966. The large depot and workshop complex at Thornbury was to survive until being largely demolished in 2012. (F.N.T. Lloyd-Jones/Online Transport Archive)

In 1935, Liverpool Corporation constructed four replacement rail scrubbers from redundant passenger cars. Nos S6-S9 were rebuilt from Nos 332, 422, 126 and 117 respectively. Three of the four were to be renumbered into the City Engineer's fleet during the Second World War, Nos S6, S7 and S9 becoming Nos 273, 283 and 287 respectively. No S8 retained its original number until withdrawal in early 1952. No 283 'pictured here with the more modern No 234 in the background' had been No S7 when converted and No 422 in the passenger fleet. As such, it was one of 300 open-top four-wheel cars – Nos 142-441 – supplied by the ERTCW during 1900 and 1901 on Brill 21E four-wheel trucks. Although threatened with scrapping in 1947, No 283 was to survive through until the final closure of the system in September 1957; it was ultimately to be scrapped in January 1958 – the last Liverpool tram so treated – and achieved the honour of serving the city for some 57 years – a record. (C. Carter/Online Transport Archive)

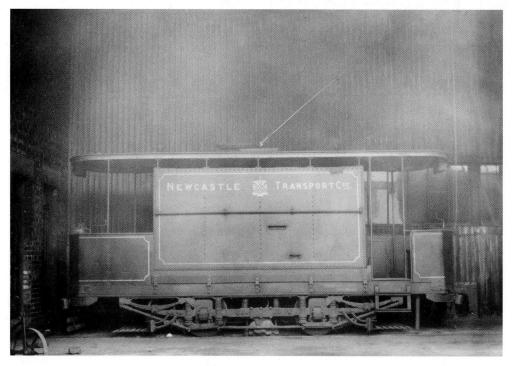

Newcastle Corporation possessed two dedicated railgrinders and water cars; this is the second of the two, No 237, pictured in February 1937. Constructed in the corporation's own workshops during 1921 on a Peckham P22 four-wheel truck, No 237 was to survive through until 1947, although it had been disused for a number of years prior to scrapping. The water tank, which was fitted with baffles (the only significant design change from the earlier car, No 166, of 1902 that had been built by the British Electric Car Co Ltd) to prevent water splashing, could hold 2,475 gallons. (Barry Cross Collection/Online Transport Archive)

Pictured in October 1949 turning into the permanent way yard at Miller Street depot is Birmingham Corporation scrubber No 9; it is wearing the 1946 blue and cream livery into which it had been repainted five months earlier. The origins of this conversion dated back to August 1921 when, following an overhaul, No 507 – one of the ERTCW-built open-top four-wheel cars acquired from the City of Birmingham Tramways Co Ltd in 1911 and originally new in 1902 – was fitted with a Brush Conaty truck and converted for works duties. By 1928, the body from No 507 was in poor condition and was scrapped in August; it was replaced by the body of sister car No 509, which had been operating as a single-deck trailer car since 1916, in December the same year. No 9 was to survive until being scrapped in March 1952. (F.N.T. Lloyd-Jones/Online Transport Archive)

A second Birmingham Corporation rail scrubber was No PW11; this was converted from No 493, another of the trams acquired from the City of Birmingham Tramways Co in 1911, and was converted to single-deck for works duties in October 1922 – the last conversion to be undertaken (sister car No 498 had been converted to scrubber No PW12 in October 1920). Both Nos PW11 and PW12 were operated with their existing Conaty four-wheel trucks; the latter was to be withdrawn in December 1932 and scrapped the following year whilst No PW11 – seen here towards the end of its life – was to survive until April 1939. (D.W.K. Jones Collection/Online Transport Archive)

LCC grinders Nos 013 and 014 had an unusual history before being converted for this work. The two, designated Class L/1 by the LCC, had their origins in surplus Brill 21E four-wheel trucks from 'B' class trams when the bodies were transferred to Rotherham Corporation in 1917. As a result of transport difficulties during the First World War, Charlton works constructed two wagon bodies that were added to the trucks to create powered wagons; the pair operated as a permanent coupled set, with platforms only at the outer ends. In about 1924, at a time when a dispute on the railways made staff travel difficult, seating was fitted and the twin-set was used for the movement of staff between Charlton and Camberwell. Eventually, later in the 1920s when conventional passenger cars were used for staff work, the two were split and converted into two rail grinders. As such, they passed to LPTB ownership in July 1933. Following the demise of other rail grinders acquired by LPTB as the system contracted, No 013 – pictured here whilst still in LCC ownership – was withdrawn in January 1938 whilst No 014 was one of three ex-LCC grinders to survive the Second World War. (Barry Cross Collection/Online Transport Archive)

In 1928, Blackpool Corporation constructed a new railgrinder – No 1 – in Rigby Road works; a second – No 2 – was added to the fleet in 1935. No 1 was renumbered 2 in 1968 and was to become No 752 in March 1972. The original No 2 was withdrawn from service in the early 1960s; it passed to the tramway museum at Crich with some of its electrical equipment being used in the restoration of Manchester No 765. After a period in use as a works vehicle at Crich, the tram's truck was used in the restoration of Chesterfield No 7. No 752 was to survive in service until the early years of the twenty-first century; it was acquired for preservation by the Heaton Park tramway in November 2008, where there are plans for its restoration to its original red livery. It is seen here in Rigby Road depot during the late summer of 1975, attached to a wire wagon. (Philip Hanson/Online Transport Archive)

In 1903, BEC supplied 3ft 6in gauge the Isle of Thanet Electric Supply Co Ltd with ten open-top cars on Brill 21E four-wheel trucks; Nos 51-60 were to be the last new trams acquired by the company and towards the end of the system's life – it was finally to close on 24 March 1937 – No 60 was to be converted into a dedicated works car, primarily for railgrinding purposes. As part of the conversion, the tram's original truck was replaced by one of the cast trucks supplied to the first batch of trams, Nos 1-20, by the US-based St Louis Car Co. The modified car is seen here alongside No 61 at the system's St Peter's depot. No 61 was constructed in 1903, probably by the company itself, on a Brush AA four-wheel truck for works duties. Employed as a water car (the tank was located behind the platforms), railgrinding and other work, No 61 appears to be in a derelict condition in this view. (D.W.K. Jones/Online Transport Archive)

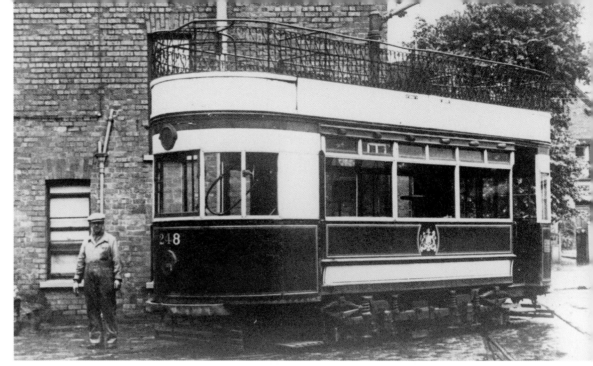

Belfast Corporation No 248, one of the fifty ex-horse trams converted to operate as an electric car, was converted into a railgrinder during the war and was fitted with vestibule ends for the purpose, although losing one staircase. It was withdrawn in January 1954. (Barry Cross Collection/Online Transport Archive)

The last new tramcar constructed for Liverpool Corporation was constructed for the city engineers' department rather than for the transport department. This was railgrinder No 234, which was completed in October 1948, and is recorded here at Edge Lane on 7 September 1956. Fitted with a purpose-built body that housed the motor-driven grinding equipment, the tram was constructed using the underframe, truck and electrical equipment from 'Standard' No 173. Less than a decade old when the system finally closed in September 1957, the corporation was initially hopeful of being able to sell the tram to one of the country's surviving systems; these hopes, however, came to nothing and No 234 was finally to be scrapped in January 1958. It and a second works car (No 283) were the last Liverpool trams to be scrapped. (R.L. Wilson/Online Transport Archive)

PERMANENT WAY CARS

Bradford Corporation's initial fleet of works cars included two tippler wagons – Nos 5 and 8 – that were both constructed in about 1905. The former is pictured here in 1913. (Barry Cross Collection/Online Transport Archive)

During 1906 and 1907, Glasgow Corporation Permanent Way Department used the equal-wheel bogies, manufactured by the Metropolitan Railway Carriage & Wagon Co Ltd of Saltley, and equipment salvaged from withdrawn 'Room & Kitchen' single-deck cars, which dated originally to 1897 and 1898, for the construction of four mineral wagons, Nos 3-6, for the movement of sand and setts. No 4 is seen here around 1908 being loaded with setts in the Transport Department's siding at Custom House Quay. Of the four, one was scrapped in the mid-1920s, two – including No 4 – had been withdrawn by the end of 1938 but one – No 6 – was to survive through until late 1949. (GCT/Ian Stewart Collection/Online Transport Archive)

In all, the Imperial Tramways Co Ltd, which operated the network of 3ft 7in gauge electric trams in Middlesbrough and Stockton-on-Tees between 1898 and 1921, possessed five works cars, including this PW car built in the company's own workshops on McGuire maximum traction bogies in 1907. Numbered 61 when new, the tram was one of those that passed to Middlesbrough Corporation when the Imperial network was divided between the various local authorities. It is pictured here in its post-1921 guise; it's uncertain whether a fleet number was carried, but there are suggestions that it was No 112 as the corporation's passenger fleet ran from 100-11/13-40. The final trams operated in Middlesbrough in 1934. (Barry Cross Collection)

Prior to its take-over by Glasgow Corporation, the Paisley & District Tramways Co possessed two dedicated works cars. No 50, built in about 1905, was a water car and track scrubber, whilst No 51 was a sand and sett wagon built by Hurst Nelson in 1907 on a Hurst Nelson 21E-type four-wheel truck. This posed view sees No 51 alongside No 52; the latter was also a product of Hurst Nelson and delivered the same year. The view was probably taken around the time that both trams were delivered, as there is a poster promoting Hurst Nelson on one of the lower-deck windows of No 52 and the passenger car was to receive an open-balcony top cover in 1910. No 51 was to survive, albeit heavily rebuilt, by both Paisley & District and by Glasgow Corporation, retaining its original fleet number until withdrawal in August 1959. (Barry Cross Collection/Online Transport Archive)

Edinburgh Corporation converted one of the four-wheel cable cars that it had taken over from the Edinburgh & District Tramways Co Ltd in 1919 – No 51 (one of a batch of 16 open-balcony trams built by the company itself between 1906 and 1911 that were the last new cable cars obtained) – into a dedicated trackwork car. Originally numbered 10 and fitted with a Peckham four-wheel truck, the tram was latterly to be No 3 and it is in this guise that the car is recorded in Shrubhill depot on 24 June 1956 – towards the end of the Edinburgh system. (Ian Crombie/Online Transport Archive)

In 1911, Southampton Corporation constructed two open wagons – Nos 100 and 101 – in its own workshops on Brill 21E four-wheel trucks. These were designed for a number of purposes, including the carrying of setts. Here, one of the duo is pictured on Shirley High Street on 20 April 1949, during the system's final year of operation. (F.E.J. Ward/Online Transport Archive)

Between January and October 1920, Birmingham Corporation constructed four specialist welding vans; these were Nos 1-4 initially but were soon renumbered PW13-PW16. The first three were fitted with Brill 21E four-wheel trucks; No 16 was initially fitted with a Conaty truck but this was later replaced by a further Brill 21E. Inside the bodies, which were constructed (as is evident in this side view) of corrugated iron, was a welding machine that was employed for the welding of rail joints during track repair and replacement. Of the four, two, Nos PW13 and PW14, were relatively short-lived, both being broken up in September 1926. No PW15 was to survive until March 1931 but the last was to survive until after the Second World War, being sold for scrap in June 1945, although was little used after 1939 as the blackout restrictions made the use of the welding kit and lighting impractical at night. (D.W.K. Jones Collection/Online Transport Archive)

Immediately after the First World War, the MET undertook a major programme of track renewal; based upon US experience, which had been investigated by the company's staff and which was cheaper than existing practice in the UK, the company authorised the construction of a track-breaking car. Converted at Hendon Works from water car No 3 at a cost of £1,678 and completed in early 1921, the new No 3 was fitted with a steam-driven pile-driving hammer at one end and was mounted on a Brush-built AA four-wheel truck. The tram was also fitted with a lengthened trolleypole for the supply of power both for the tram's motor as well as the winch that lowered and raised the winch that supported the hammer. The hammer itself was operated by steam generated from a small vertical steam engine carried on a small, unpowered, four-wheel wagon. The complete ensemble – pictured in this view – was destined to have a relatively short life in this guise; two years after its completion, the winch and hammer were transferred to a new bogie car. This itself was only to survive in operation until the mid-1920s, being replaced by pneumatic drills, although the tram was to survive longer in store; its exact scrapping date is uncertain. (Barry Cross Collection/Online Transport Archive)

In 1906, Plymouth Corporation acquired six demi cars from Brush – Nos 37-42 – that were fitted with Brush AA four-wheel trucks for use on the West Hoe to North Road station route. In 1922, the last of the batch, No 42, was converted to act as a welding car, in which guise it is pictured here towards the end of its life (its condition would indicate that its working career had ended). The remaining five cars were all scrapped in 1924. (Maurice J. O'Connor/NTM)

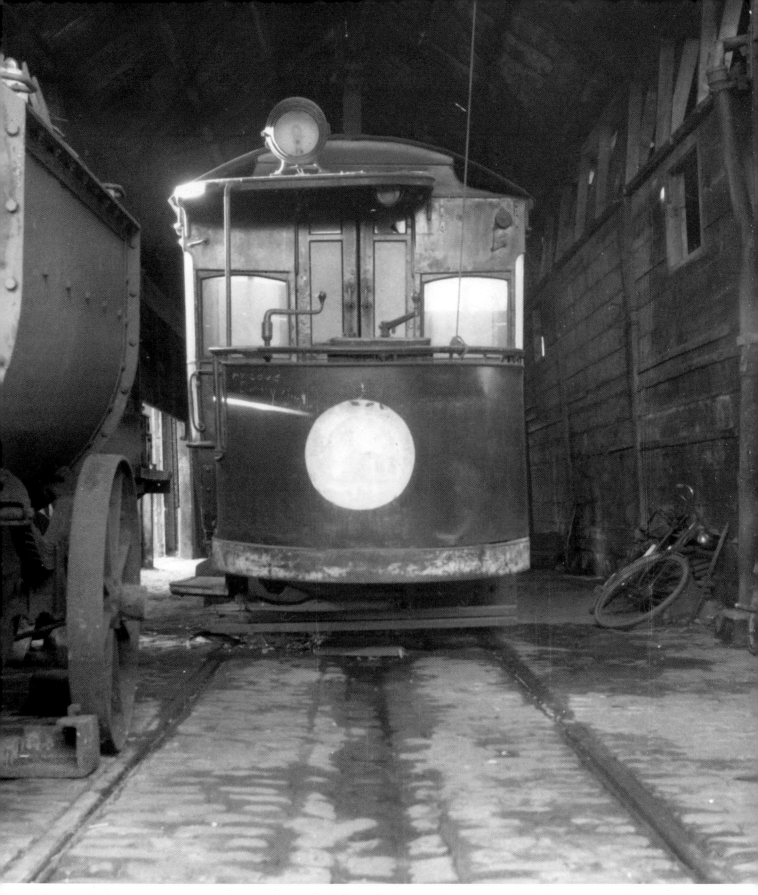

Pictured inside the corporation's Highfield Road permanent way depot in December 1948 alongside a tar wagon is Southampton Corporation's welding car. This was originally passenger car No 22, which was one of a batch of nine open-top trams built by G.F. Milnes & Co – Nos 21-29 – that were fitted with Brill 21E four-wheel trucks. No 22 was converted to a welding car in 1928 and renumbered 105E at that time. The depot had originally been a horse bus depot operated by the Southampton Tramways Co and passed to the corporation with the rest of the company's assets in 1898. (F.E.J. Ward/Online Transport Archive)

Blackpool Corporation No 5, seen here outside Rigby Road depot, was the second works car to carry this fleet number. It was converted in 1936 from No 114. This car had originally been Blackpool & Fleetwood Tramroad Co No 40 and was one of a batch of four – Nos 38-41 – supplied to the company by UEC on the same manufacturer's M&G-type bogies in 1914; these were the last new trams acquired by the company and all four passed to the corporation on 1 January 1920. In service until 1960, the tram was restored to its original condition that year as part of the celebrations of the 75th anniversary of the original conduit tramway. Following this, it was preserved and now forms part of the collection held by the National Tramway Museum. (F.E.J. Ward/Online Transport Archive)

During the Second World War, three of the ex-Blackpool & Fleetwood single-deck crossbench trams were converted for works duties. No 132 was converted into a permanent way car in around 1942. The tram, seen here outside Copse Road depot, was one of a batch of ten – Nos 1-10 – that was supplied to the Blackpool & Fleetwood Tramroad Co in 1898. Built by G.F. Milnes & Co and fitted with the same manufacturer's bogies, the ten cars were renumbered 126-35 following the corporation take-over on 1 January 1920. Two other cars from the batch were also converted for works duties. No 1 (as No 126) was also used as a permanent way car (No 3) after approximately 1942, whilst No 2 (No 127) was used as a snow plough. The latter was restored in 1960 as Blackpool & Fleetwood No 2 and was subsequently preserved; it is now part of the National Tramway Museum collection. No 6 was last used in 1955 and was subsequently scrapped. (Phil Tatt/Online Transport Archive)

A number of Blackpool Corporation trams have, over the years, been converted from passenger duty to act as staff cars for those employed on PW work. In April 1965, one of the batch of original English Electric-built railcoaches, No 221 (new in February 1934 and fitted with English Electric-built bogies), which had been withdrawn and stored in 1963, was to emerge as works car No 5. It was to remain on works duties until October 1971 when it was withdrawn again, this time for rebuilding into one of the 13 OMO trams that the corporation put into service between October 1972 and June 1976. Retaining its No 5 as an OMO car, the rebuilt tram re-entered service in November 1972. It was to remain in service in this rebuilt guise until withdrawal in 1993; subsequently the tram was preserved and now forms part of the National Tramway Museum collection, albeit in store and in an unrestored condition. It is pictured here in Rigby Road on 22 May 1966, shortly after its renumbering for works duties. (R.L. Wilson/Online Transport Archive)

REVENUE-EARNING NON-PASSENGER AND FREIGHT CARS

Recognising the need to move coal by rail to the power station that supplied the line, the Snaefell Mountain Railway constructed a seventh power car – No 7 (nicknamed 'Maria') – in 1896, using a frame supplied by G.F. Milnes & Co alongside local sourced material. Unusually, the vehicle did not receive its own bogies but, used primarily during the winter months, received the equipment from one of the passenger cars – normally No 5. After the closure of the power station in the mid-1920s, No 7 was retained for use as a PW car during the winter months, being stored without equipment – as seen here alongside the derrick for use on the overhead and a match wagon – during the summer months. Withdrawn in 1955, the remains of No 7 were finally scrapped in 1995. (Geoffrey Morant Collection/Online Transport Archive)

The only electric tramway in Cornwall was the Camborne & Redruth, which was owned by the Urban Electric Supply Co Ltd; this 3½-mile long 3ft 6in gauge line provided a passenger service, which also carried parcels and post, between the two towns but much of its traffic was derived from the movement of tin ore from the mines at East Pool and Wheal Agar as well as the tin crushing works at Tolvaddon Downs; the last named was served by a short – half-mile – branch north from the depot. Alongside the eight passenger cars, the company also employed two four-wheel electric locomotives supplied by G.F. Milnes & Co in 1903, alongside eight mineral wagons. One of the locomotives is pictured with a wagon when virtually new. Although passenger services over the line ceased on 29 September 1927, mineral traffic continued until 1934, when the service was replaced by an aerial ropeway. (W.S. Eades Collection/Online Transport Archive)

The 3ft 6in gauge Great Orme was originally designed to carry passengers and freight, including parcels, up and down the Great Orme. Amongst the unusual traffic catered for were coffins from the town to the station at Halfway for interment at St Tudno's churchyard. In order to cater for the non-passenger traffic, three unpowered goods wagons – Nos 1-3 – were supplied by Hurst Nelson, the company that also constructed the four passenger cars used on the line. The wagons could either be placed in front of one of the passenger cars and pushed up the gradient or the cable could be detached from the passenger car and attached to the wagon. Either way, the traffic was relatively short-lived and ceased completely by 1911. This view shows No 3 stabled outside the terminus in Llandudno. (Barry Cross Collection/Online Transport Archive)

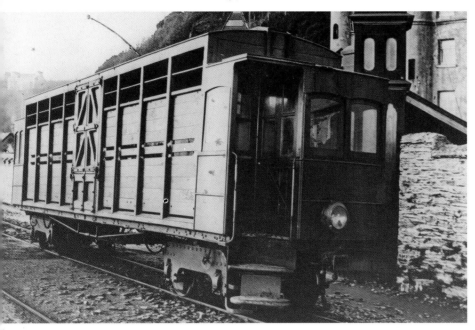

Whilst the carriage of mineral or coal traffic by electric tramway was relatively rare, the movement of livestock was very restricted and probably limited to the Manx Electric Railway. In 1903, the MER converted No 12 to handle the traffic. The following year, two dedicated unpowered wagons – Nos 24 and 25 – were added to the fleet with traffic operating from Ramsey and Laxey to a dedicated docks at Derby Castle. This view of No 12 was taken prior to 1912 as in that year, No 12 was converted into an unpowered trailer and renumbered 22. After the First World War, the livestock traffic declined and the two 1904-built wagons were rebuilt for stone traffic. No 22 lingered on until 1927 when it was scrapped; the tram's chassis had been corroded beyond the point of economic repair.
(Barry Cross Collection/Online Transport Archive)

Pictured at the Derby Castle terminus of the Manx Electric Railway is large mail van No 16. This was one of two completed at Derby Castle in 1908. From construction through to 1955, No 16 carried 'Royal Mail' lettering. The wagon was taken out of service in the late 1970s – the loss of the mail traffic was one of the factors behind the threat of closure to the Laxey to Ramsey section at the time – and stored at Ramsey until 1992. Following restoration to its post-1955 condition, No 16 re-entered service for display purposes in mid-2015. No 15 was less fortunate; it was scrapped in 1944 following damage in an accident the previous year.
(John McCann/Online Transport Archive)

Pictured in 1904 when new, Huddersfield No 72 was one of two coal trucks – the other being No 71 – that were supplied by G.C. Milnes, Voss & Co Ltd. Fitted with Brush radial four-wheel trucks, the two trams were designed to carry coal from the coal shutes operated by Martin, Sons & Co Ltd at Hillhouse to three mills that were situated on the Outlane route. Designed to carry ten tons of coal on each journey, operational experience resulted in modifications to the trams during their lives; this included the relocation of the trolleypole and the insertion of half-circular boards behind the platforms in order to prevent coal falling onto the platforms. The two trams were to be subsequently renumbered 1 and 2 and were to survive until sold for scrap in December 1934. (Barry Cross Collection/Online Transport Archive)

Manchester Corporation was one of a number of operators that offered a parcels service. In all, seven four-wheel trams were completed for this traffic. The first three entered service in 1905 and this view records one of that trio, probably No 1 as it is pictured without canopies over the two platforms; whilst photographs of No 1 in this condition exist, there are no known photographs of the other two. Nos 1-5 were four-wheel cars (No 1 with a cantilever truck and Nos 2-5 eventually on 21E trucks) whilst Nos 6 and 7 were fitted to 22E type bogies. Apart from use for parcels traffic, the seven cars were also used for PW duties; with the cessation of the former work, all seven were used exclusively for PW work, often for the movement of bags of sand to depots for use in the sand boxes of the passenger fleet. Only two – Nos 5 and 7 – were to survive until 1939. (Barry Cross Collection/Online Transport Archive)

In November 1905, the Birmingham & Midland Tramways Joint Committee commenced the operation of a parcels service across its network. This view of parcels car No 6 towing an open trailer was taken in 1917 on Tipton Road, Dudley, when the tram was new. The view postdates the rebranding of the operation as 'Tramways & Motor Express' which took place during the winter of 1914/15 when the service was co-ordinated with that offered by the Birmingham & Midland Motor Omnibus Co (Midland Red) and extended to include general goods. No 7 was constructed in the committee's own workshops at Tividale on a Brill 21E four-wheel truck. (Tramway & Railway World/Barry Cross Collection/Online Transport Archive)

In all, between 1906 and 1922 Leeds Corporation acquired eighteen heavy freight – or 'Tippler' – wagons. Initially, the first two were designed to provide a service to a goods siding – never constructed – on Cardigan Road and further batches followed as traffic requirements dictated. No 8 is seen here loading at the wharf on the Leeds-Liverpool Canal. No 8 was one of seven – No 3-9 – that were new in August 1910. All of the 'Tippler' cars were completed in Kirkstall Road Works; Nos 1-12 were fitted with Peckham Cantilever four-wheel trucks, whilst Nos 13-17 were fitted with Hurst Nelson-built 21E four-wheel trucks and No 18 with a Brush Cantilever truck. The trucks on Nos 13-17 were replaced by Peckham Cantilever trucks by 1923 when rail-grinding equipment was also fitted. Each hopper was designed to carry a maximum of 5½ tons and was removable to permit the vehicles to operate as a flat truck or to carry equipment. All were in stock at December 1931 but their use declined thereafter. The last, relegated to permanent way duties, was No 4; this survived minus its hoppers 'but by now fitted with a bow collector' until 1948. The electric crane was one of two supplied to the corporation by Joseph Booth & Bros of Rodley; this one in 1910 and the second in early 1922. The somewhat basic protection for the operator was soon replaced by a cab constructed out of match boarding. This crane was to survive – latterly in a poor condition – in the yard at Sovereign Street – until the final abandonment of the system in November 1959; it was scrapped three months later. (Barry Cross Collection/Online Transport Archive)

Pictured in the latter days of the Birmingham & Midland Tramways Joint Committee's parcels service at the depot on Lionel Street in Birmingham, is No 4. The tram is seen with a horse-drawn van as parcels are transferred between the two. No 4 was also constructed at Tividale in about 1913, probably utilising the frame of a withdrawn tram and a reused 'Lord Baltimore' truck from a withdrawn single-deck tram originally supplied by the ERTCW in 1900. The use of the branding 'Tramways & Motorbus Express' again confirms this as a post-1915 view. (Tramway & Railway World/Barry Cross Collection/Online Transport Archive)

In all, Dublin United Tramways operated a fleet of some seventy wagons; the majority of these, however, were to be scrapped in the late 1920s following the cessation of freight operation in 1927. No 68, pictured here, was to be the last survivor, being used in Spa Road Works until the 1960s as a skip for rubbish. Here, the car is recorded with No 23; this was another attendance car – see No 22 on page 30 – that dated back to at least 1910. Fitted with a Peckham truck, No 23 was to survive into the 1930s. (Barry Cross Collection/Online Transport Archive)

Although there had been proposals twice prior to the outbreak of the First World War for the operation of coal trams in Southend-on-Sea, it was not until February 1915 that such a service was introduced. For the work, three motorised hopper wagons – Nos 1-3 – were constructed by the corporation using 21E trucks from passenger cars Nos 5, 8 and 26 (which received new Peckham radial trucks in their place). The motors for the coal hoppers were also reused from Nos 5, 8 and 26, which again received newer replacement motors. The trio was employed to run from a coal jetty (Corporation Loading Pier completed with its loop in 1913), located immediately to the east of the famous pier, to the depot and generating station on London Road. The first of the trio to be withdrawn was No 3; this was taken out of service in March 1931 as a result of the gradual run-down in the amount of coal transported to the corporation's power station as an increasing amount of power was purchased from outside suppliers. The surviving two cars – pictured here with their twin hoppers – were to survive through until later in 1931, when they were both offered for sale as the movement of coal ceased. (Barry Cross Collection/Online Transport Archive)

SNOW PLOUGHS AND SALT WAGONS

Dundee Corporation was one of a number of operators that utilised redundant steam tram locomotives as snow ploughs. One of the quartet that Dundee converted in 1902 is pictured with the snow plough prominent. (Barry Cross Collection/Online Transport Archive)

Between 1900 and 1909, Leeds Corporation acquired five snow sweepers. The first of these – No 1 illustrated here in Sovereign Street yard in about 1904 – was supplied with a Brush body fitted to a Brill four-wheel truck in early 1900. The remaining four completed were all provided with bodies constructed by the corporation on Brill four-wheel trucks. (D.W.K. Jones Collection/ Online Transport Archive)

In about 1901, the Bristol Tramways & Carriage Co was supplied with two snow ploughs by the McGuire Manufacturing Co Ltd of Bury in Lancashire; these were fitted on the manufacturer's rigid frame four-wheel trucks. No 1 – the numbers were not actually carried – was the smaller of the two and operated as both a snow plough and a brush car. In addition, three passenger cars were also converted to works duties. No 92 'in 1923' was an additional snow plough, whilst Nos 86 (in 1920) and 97 (in 1929) were converted to act as railgrinders. (Barry Cross Collection/Online Transport Archive)

The larger of the snow ploughs supplied to the Bristol Tramways & Carriage Co in about 1901 was No 2 – again unnumbered – and this car was to survive until the end of the system in 1941. It is pictured here towards the end of its working life. (Barry Cross Collection/Online Transport Archive)

Wallasey Corporation No 26, seen here after the system's abandonment on 30 November 1933, at Seaview Road, had originally been supplied by ERTCW on a Brill 21E in 1902 as a water car. Three years after delivery, it was decided to rebuild the tram as a stores car and snow plough. This was achieved by the removal of the water tank and by the addition of a van body. During summer months, it was used for the secure transfer of takings from New Brighton to the depot. (Barry Cross Collection/Online Transport Archive)

Alongside No 26, Wallasey Corporation also possessed a sole salt wagon; this unnumbered vehicle was supplied by UEC in February 1911. Normally towed by No 26, or by one of the passenger cars of the Nos 33-35 batch, the wagon was to survive through to the end of the system in 1933. (Barry Cross Collection/Online Transport Archive)

Between 1900 and 1909, Leeds Corporation acquired five snow sweepers – Nos 1-5 – that were fitted with Brill rigid frame four-wheel trucks. No 1, built by Brush, was delivered in 1900; Nos 2 and 3 in 1902 and the last two in 1909 and were constructed in Kirkstall Road works. When new, the quintet was unnumbered but subsequently were noted in a white or cream livery with black numerals; latterly – as demonstrated in this view of No 3 – the cars were painted in grey with black numerals. This view shows to good effect the Brill rotating broom used to facilitate the clearing of fresh snow once the initial drifts had been cleared. (F.E.J. Ward/Online Transport Archive)

Oldham Corporation possessed two dedicated works cars, both of which were new in 1903: No 38 was a water car, whilst No 3, portrayed here on 28 June 1922, was originally a snow plough. There is some uncertainty as to the manufacturer of No 3's body – it was either the corporation itself or ERTCW – but, like No 38, it was fitted with a Brill 21E four-wheel truck. No 3 – used latterly for the movement of welding equipment having been converted in 1923 – was scrapped in December 1931 although No 38 was not to be dismantled until September 1942. (Barry Cross Collection/Online Transport Archive)

Sheffield Corporation converted seven of its early single-deck passenger cars into snow ploughs between 1913 and 1921; one of the last to be so treated was No 39, which had originally been built by G.F. Milnes & Co in 1899, which was modified for works duties in October 1921. The tram was to be renumbered 95 in 1924 and to 102 two years later; it was to gain its final identity as No 362 in 1929. Although four of the conversions were to be withdrawn during the 1920s, three, including No 362, were to soldier on until the final years of the Sheffield system. No 362 was withdrawn in May 1956 and No 363 in April the following year; both were to be scrapped. More fortunate was No 354; this was to survive through until 1960 and was restored to its original condition, as No 46, to appear in the system's closing ceremony. After withdrawal, No 46 was acquired for preservation and now forms part of the National Tramway Museum collection. (Barry Cross Collection/Online Transport Archive)

Between 1900 and 1902, Aberdeen Corporation converted 13 of the horse trams that it had acquired from the Aberdeen District Tramways Co into electric cars fitted with Brill 21E four-wheel trucks. The numbering of the trams is uncertain – Aberdeen numbered its initial trams by route and these cars may subsequently have been numbered 34-46 – but latterly they were Nos 57-65 – with long canopies – and Nos 66-69 – with short canopies. Nos 66-69 were rebuilt as salt cars and snow ploughs prior to 1910, with the remainder – including this car that bears a crudely painted No 58 on the side – being converted to salt cars during the 1920s.
(W.A. Camwell/NTM)

Aberdeen Corporation possessed two works cars numbered 4A; the first of these, pictured here towards the end of its life, was one of the original eight electric cars delivered to the corporation in 1899. Nos 1-8 were constructed by Brush on Brill 21E four-wheel trucks for the opening of the route to Woodside; in around 1930, No 4 was converted into a salt car and was to be renumbered 4A in 1936. The second No 4A was converted in 1948 from No 56, a BEC-built tram again on a Brill 21E truck dating originally to 1903, to act as a railgrinder. (Harry Luff Collection/Online Transport Archive)

In all, Manchester Corporation possessed 20 salt trailers; these were generally fitted with unpowered Brill 21E four-wheel trucks and were propelled, as illustrated here, by being pushed by service cars. As the system declined during the 1930s, the majority of the trailers were withdrawn but five were still extant by the end of the Second World War. (Barry Cross Collection/ Online Transport Archive)

Two of Sheffield Corporation's fleet of snow ploughs are pictured outside Shoreham Street depot. In the foreground is stores car No 361. This had originally been passenger car No 99 – one of 15 built by Brush (Nos 89-103) that were fitted with Brill 21E trucks – and new in September 1900. It was converted into a snow plough in November 1921 and was to be renumbered 361 in 1929. It survived in service until April 1960. Behind is No 357; this was originally an open-top double-deck car, No 225, that was new in February 1904; this was also constructed by Brush, one of 45 – Nos 104-23 and 219-43 – with Brill 21E trucks. All were to be fitted with top covers between 1903 and 1913. Converted into a snow plough and renumbered 278 in August 1933, it was to become No 357 during 1937. No 357 was one of the works cars that was to survive through to the final closure of the system in October 1960. (R.W.A. Jones/Online Transport Archive)

In 1925, Stockport Corporation converted redundant passenger car No 6 into a dedicated snow plough and salt car, No 102, as illustrated here. No 6 had originally been one of the first batch of 10 open-top electric trams supplied by ERTCW on Brill 21E four-wheel trucks to the corporation in 1901. Whilst a number of the type received top covers during 1911 and 1912, No 6 was not one of them. Prior to the conversion, the corporation had used two converted horse trams as salt trailers. (Geoffrey Morant Collection/Online Transport Archive)

Two of Gateshead & District's works cars await disposal following the closure of the system in 1951. Closest to the camera is snow plough No 45; this had originally started life as an open-top double-deck car, No 25, that was one of a batch of 25 – Nos 21-45 – supplied by ERTCW in 1901 on Brill 21E four-wheel trucks. It was rebuilt as a single-deck car in 1923 and subsequently renumbered 45, being used latterly as a snow plough. Behind is No 51A; this was the only tram built specifically for works duties on the Gateshead system. When built by ERTCW on a Brill 21E truck, No 51 was designed as a water car; renumbered 51A in 1925, the tram was subsequently converted to operate as either a rail grinder or snow plough. (F.N.T. Lloyd-Jones/Online Transport Archive)

In 1902, ERTCW supplied Stockport Corporation with a batch of fourteen open-top double-deck cars – Nos 11-24 – fitted with Brill 21E four-wheel trucks. All bar No 13 had been rebuilt with some form of top cover by 1923 and, in 1927, No 3 was withdrawn and converted into a snow plough. It is pictured here in that condition. In 1944, No 13 was reconditioned and fitted with a top cover, re-entering passenger service as No 45 – a rare example of a works car being reconverted back into passenger use. It was to survive in service until final withdrawal in 1949. (Barry Cross Collection/Online Transport Archive)

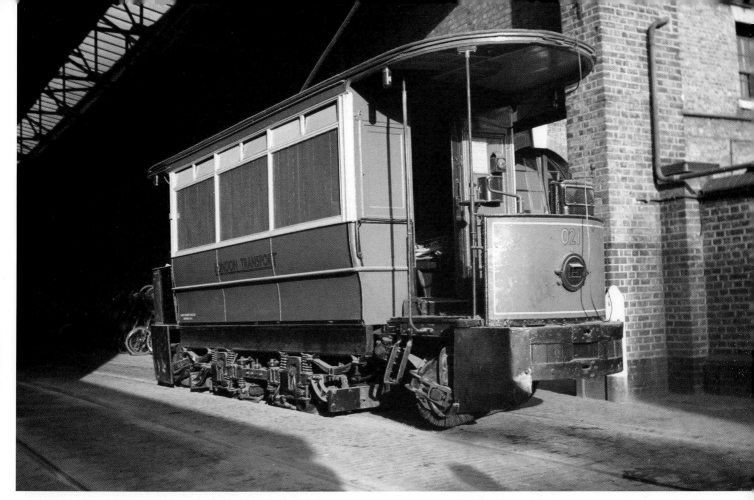

Between 1927 and 1935, the LCC converted thirty-nine old passenger cars from Classes B and C into either snow brooms (Nos 016-36) or snow ploughs (Nos 037-54). With the exception of No 045, which operated for a period in double-deck form, all were cut down to single-deck for the work. All passed to the LPTB in July 1933 and a number were to survive through to the post-war years. Under LPTB ownership, Nos 037, 040-43/48 were converted from snow ploughs to snow brooms and replaced similar cars inherited from other constituent operators. By the start of the final elimination of London's trams in Operation Tramaway from 1950 onwards, the number of works cars employed by the LTE had been reduced to 31 stores and snow brooms in total. No 021, which had originally been Class B No 168 (one of a batch of 100 – Nos 102-201 – supplied by ERTCW on Brill 21E trucks in 1903), is seen here; this car was to survive until towards the end of the system, not being scrapped at Penhall Road until April 1952. (Phil Tatt/Online Transport Archive)

In early 1950, four of LT's surviving works cars were recorded at Telford Avenue awaiting their next duties. Closest to the camera in this view were Nos 025 and 034; beyond were Nos 033 and 022. The latter was to be preserved on withdrawal and, eventually, restored as LCC No 106 and is now resident at the National Tramway Museum. The decision to convert the first thirteen of 'B' class cars was made in late 1926 and the contract for the supply of the snow plough equipment was given to the Kilmarnock Engineering Co. The conversion work, which included the loss of the top deck and the adding of brackets to support the platform canopies – essential once the stairs had been removed – was undertaken at Charlton Works. The first were introduced in 1927 – just in time for heavy snow that winter – and approval for the conversion of a further seven trams was given in January 1928. No 025 – ex-No 125 – was part of the first batch and No 034 – ex-No 144 – was the penultimate of the second batch. It was estimated that the conversion cost about £172 per tram. (Peter N. Williams/Online Transport Archive)

At the commencement of Operation Tramaway in 1950, the LTE possessed seventeen snow brooms –
Nos 016-26/28/33-37 – but as the system contracted, so the number was reduced. In April 1951, two
of the survivors – with No 018 closest to the camera – await the attention of the scrapmen at Penhall
Road. No 018 had originally been 'B' class No 195 and had been converted into a snow broom in 1927.
(W.J. Wyse/LRTA (London Area) Collection/Online Transport Archive)

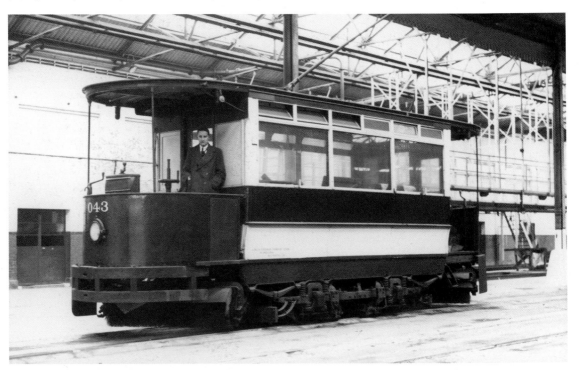

In 1931, the LCC decided to convert eighteen of the then redundant 'C' class double-deck cars into
additional snow ploughs. These 100 trams had originally been built by Brush on Brill 21E trucks and were
new in 1904. No 043 – seen here in Finchley depot when newly modified – had originally been No 241 and
was converted in 1935 after the creation of the LPTB. Like a number of the snow brooms No 043 was
withdrawn just prior to the Second World War as a result of the contraction of the London systems.

(W.A. Camwell/National Tramway Museum)

LCC No 045 was the only one of the ex-passenger cars converted into snow ploughs to operate in this role whilst retaining its upper deck. As No 215, it had originally been a 'C' class tram, one of one hundred – Nos 202-301 – built by Brush on Brill 21E four-wheel trucks. It was taken out of service in August 1936. (D.W.K. Jones Collection/Online Transport Archive)

During October 1932, Leeds Corporation converted nine old passenger cars into snow ploughs. Nos 6-14 had been Nos 166A, 168A, 154A, 157A, 136A, 151A, 162A, 161A and 182A respectively. Pictured outside Becket Street depot on 26 March 1938, still bearing evidence of its former fleet number on its side, chalked by the photographer, is No 12. All nine of the converted trams had originally been supplied by British Thomson-Houston from a batch of 50 (Nos 133-82 – although Nos 143-54 were rejected and returned to the manufacturer) constructed using Brush bodies on Peckham Cantilever four-wheel trucks and new originally in 1899. Open-top when delivered, all received top covers during 1912. (W.A. Camwell/National Tramway Museum)

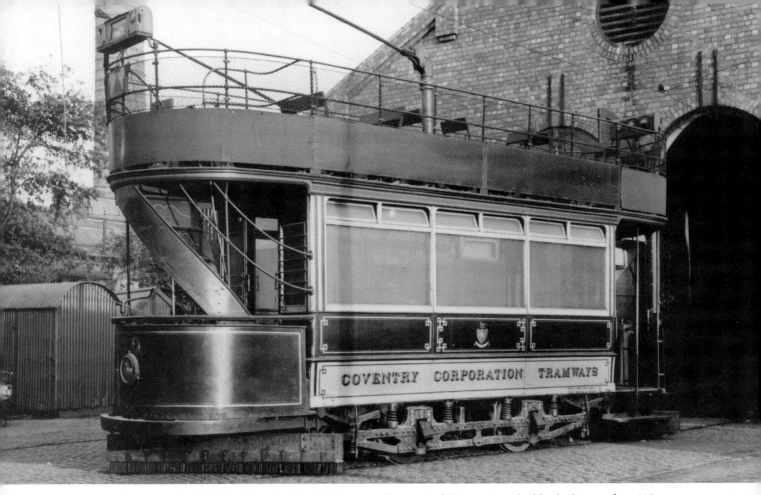

In 1904, the Coventry Electric Tramways Co acquired 12 open-top double-deck trams from Wigan Corporation; numbered 19-30 by the company and, after 1912, by Coventry Corporation, two of the batch – Nos 27 and 30 – were converted into snow ploughs following withdrawal in 1933. Here, the latter is seen outside Priestley's Bridge depot on 22 September 1938. This car was to be seriously damaged during the air raid of 14 November 1940 that resulted in the closure of the Coventry system. (W.A. Camwell/National Tramway Museum)

A wartime (or immediately post-war) view – as evinced by the white-painted underframe – sees Bradford Corporation snow plough No S.3 hard at work in wintry conditions. The Bradford system possessed the highest tram terminus in Britain – at Queensbury (converted to bus operation on 5 November 1949) – and retained a sizeable fleet of snow ploughs until towards the end of the system; in all, some eight survived post-war, with the last not being taken out of service until the final closure in May 1950. No S.3 was one of two converted from passenger cars in November 1933 and had originally been No 155 when new from G.F. Milnes & Co in 1902; renumbered 123 in 1921, the car was to survive as a snow plough until final withdrawal in June 1949. (Barry Cross Collection/Online Transport Archive)

Also converted into a snow plough by Bradford Corporation in November 1933 was No 133. This was another of the G.F. Milnes & Co-built trams of 1902 but had been fitted with a 'Bailey'-style top-cover by 1905. Originally fitted with Brush A four-wheel trucks, this was replaced by a Hurst Nelson-built 21E. Following conversion, the tram emerged as No S.4 and is pictured here outside the depot at Horton Bank Top on 22 August 1949. Unlike No S.3, No S.4 was to survive through to the final closure of the system in May 1950. (John Meredith/Online Transport Archive)

Sunderland Corporation converted two ex-passenger cars into snow ploughs, No 59 becoming No D in 1938 and No 65 becoming No C two years later. The latter is pictured outside Hylton Road depot on 19 April 1947. No 65 had originally been one of a batch of 10 open-top trams – Nos 56-65 – that were supplied by the ERTCW in 1902. Originally fitted with Brill 21E four-wheel trucks, No 65 was one of five fitted with replacement Peckham P22 trucks when rebuilt as fully-enclosed between 1926 and 1929. Both Nos C and D were to survive in service through until 1951. (John Meredith/Online Transport Archive)

During the Second World War, Liverpool Corporation converted a number of passenger cars for non-revenue earning purposes. Eight – Nos 306, 507/43/58/61/64/66/75 – were modified to act as mobile decontaminant cars in the event of gas attacks early in the war whilst, from 1942, additional trams were converted into snow ploughs. In 1946, No 566, one of those earlier converted for ARP work, was converted into a snow plough. As the system contracted, so the number of ploughs required was reduced and No 566 was one of those ploughs withdrawn in early 1952, having last been used in January that year. It is seen here outside Edge Lane depot awaiting disposal; by this date all Liverpool passenger trams were painted green, but survivors such as No 566 still retained the earlier lined out red livery – albeit in a fairly care-worn condition. (Phil Tatt/Online Transport Archive)

By the end of 1952, Liverpool Corporation had converted four withdrawn Priestly 'Standards' into replacement snow ploughs – Nos SP.1-SP.4. These had originally been Nos 30, 703, 684 and 646 respectively and were from a large class of 321 trams constructed between 1922 and 1933. With the contraction of the system, the quartet had a relatively short life in their new guise. No SP.3 was the first to be withdrawn, in September 1955 (although it was used to shunt withdrawn cars at Edge Lane for scrap thereafter until it met its own fate), with Nos SP.2 and SP.4 following in May 1957. The former was to survive until after the system's closure, again being used to shunt withdrawn cars. The last of the quartet, No SP.1 – seen here at Edge Lane in 1956 – was to survive until the system's closure in September 1957 and was one of the last Liverpool trams to be scrapped, not finally succumbing until January 1958. (R.L. Wilson/Online Transport Archive)

STEAM AND ELECTRIC LOCOMOTIVES

In 1900, the Manx Electric Railway constructed a twelve-ton steeple cab locomotive – No 23 – at Derby Castle to handle the line's stone traffic. Never possessing its own trucks, No 23 was fitted with those from passenger car No 17 when required. However, the original No 23 was seriously damaged in a collision on 24 January 1914 and its remains were then stored. During the 1920s, as freight traffic increased, No 23 was revived during the winter of 1925/26 but in a very different guise to its original condition. The original cab was used on a new underframe with MER-built six-ton wagon bodies mounted on either side. The vehicle still lacked dedicated bogies; when required in service, the bogies from No 33 were usually used. Heavily used during the war when the RAF airfields at Andreas and Jurby were rebuilt, by 1944 it was redundant and stored on a set of ex-trailer bogies. It is recorded here in that condition. Acquired for preservation after many years in store in 1978, No 23 is at the time of writing in store at Laxey. (W.J. Wyse/LRTA (London Area) Collection/Online Transport Archive)

The LCC acquired the site of the future tramway repair works at Charlton in 1908 and the facility was opened on 6 March 1909. Two years later, the site was extended and a connection to the main line railway authorised. To operate the line, the LCC purchased an 0-6-0ST – No 1 – second-hand from the Southern Sewer Construction Co. The locomotive, which had been built by Andrew Barclay, Sons & Co Ltd of Kilmarnock (Works' No 991), was new originally in 1904. The works were taken over by the LPTB on 1 July 1933; the locomotive, however, was sold the same year. (Barry Cross Collection/Online Transport Archive)

In 1905, following the electrification of the 3ft 6in gauge Dublin & Lucan Electric Railway, an electric locomotive was acquired from British Thomson-Houston with the body constructed by UEC on a Brill 21E four-wheel truck. No 17 was designed to haul freight traffic over the seven-mile line, being capable of hauling up to 18 tons of traffic at 10mph up a gradient of 1 in 20. The locomotive was to survive in this guise until it was rebuilt in 1918. (Barry Cross Collection/Online Transport Archive)

In 1918, the Dublin & Lucan Electric Railway rebuilt its existing electric locomotive and renumbered it 26. The resulting vehicle had a replacement body constructed at the company's own workshops at Conyngham Road, again fitted on a Brill 21E truck. As can be seen in this view, benches were provided behind both vestibules, offering seating accommodation for up to 10 passengers. The rebuilt car was, however, to have a relatively short life. The company went bankrupt in early 1925 and all services ceased on 29 January of that year. Although the line was subsequently rebuilt – to the 5ft 3in gauge – and reopened by Dublin United Tramways, none of the 3ft 6in gauge cars were retained. (Barry Cross Collection/Online Transport Archive)

First recorded in 1910, Dublin United Tramway's No 24 was used as a haulage wagon and locomotive. Normally based at Ballsbridge depot, it is seen here alongside four-wheel 'Standard' No 44 and bogie 'Standard' No 284. No 24 was one of a handful of DUT works cars to survive the Second World War. It was to be scrapped in 1949. The other post-war survivors were water car No 4, engineering car No 31 (see page 39), Stores wagon No 51 and grinder No 73. Also to survive was the unnumbered directors car; this was sold privately in 1950 and its remains are now preserved. (F.N.T. Lloyd-Jones/Online Transport Archive)

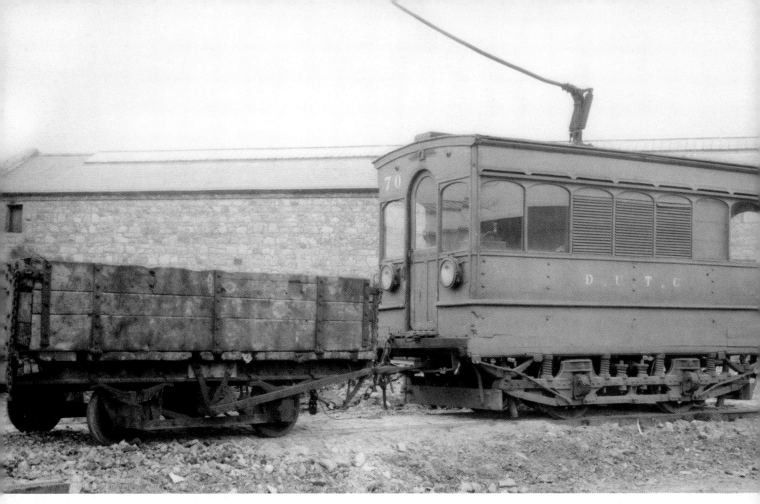

Regarded by Dublin United Tramways as a locomotive, No 70 – seen here at the PW yard at Donnybrook with wagon No 16 – was originally passenger car No 70. This was one of 86 ex-horse cars converted to electric traction between 1897 and 1900. Fitted with a Peckham truck, No 70 was to be modified for works duties in 1911. Although its exact withdrawal date is uncertain, it was employed in the late 1930s. (Barry Cross Collection/Online Transport Archive)

A further Dublin United Tramways locomotive was No 76; this was to survive through until about 1940. (Barry Cross Collection/Online Transport Archive)

Burnley Corporation possessed two 4ft 0in gauge works cars: No 1 that dated to 1903; and No 2, seen here when new, in 1925. Constructed by the corporation itself and classified as locomotives, the two were primarily water cars, but could also operate as snow ploughs or railgrinders as well as haul wagons if and when required. The second locomotive was destined to have a relatively short operational life; the process of converting the Burnley system to bus operation commenced in 1932 and the final closure came, following the creation of the Burnley, Colne & Nelson Joint Transport Committee, on 7 May 1935. (Barry Cross Collection/ Online Transport Archive)

In 1927, English Electric supplied an 0-4-0 electric locomotive to Blackpool Corporation. Initially, this was employed to haul coal wagons from the LMS transfer sidings behind Copse Road depot in Fleetwood – where this view was taken – to new sidings at Thornton Gate, a distance of 2½ miles. Following the cessation of this traffic in 1949, the locomotive was transferred to works duties, being used to haul the weedkilling tram (No 7 – see page 134) and other such work. The locomotive was originally painted red, but was to be repainted green – in which livery it is recorded – in 1938. Withdrawn in September 1963, the locomotive was to be stored in Bispham depot for two years before being acquired for preservation at the Tramway Museum at Crich on 28 January 1966. Slightly modified in preservation, the locomotive is now used at the NTM for depot shunting. (Phil Tatt/Online Transport Archive)

Sunderland Corporation's power station, situated behind Hylton Road depot, was opened in 1895 and was extended in 1926 and again in 1941. Eventually, the site was provided with seven wooden and one concrete cooling tower. In order to move coal to the power station, the corporation employed an electric locomotive, new in 1900, that ran south from the power station, past the depot and over the Circle route using a level crossing, before terminating in sidings just south of Hylton Road. (Phil Tatt/Online Transport Archive)

Although a number of tramways owned electric locomotives for operation over their own metals, Glasgow was unusual in that it permitted the operation of a third-party's locomotive and stock to operate on its track. In 1940, Dick, Kerr supplied a type 3B four-wheel, Works' No 1131, locomotive to the Fairfield Shipbuilding & Engineering Co Ltd; this was one of a number of similar locomotives supplied to the domestic market between 1920 and 1951. Used to move freight traffic from BR's goods yard at Govan to the shipyard, the locomotive's bow collector was replaced by twin trolleybooms for continued use once the route over which it operated was converted to trolleybus operation. With the closure of the Glasgow trolleybus system in 1968, the locomotive was to become redundant. Subsequently preserved, it now forms part of the collection of the Scottish Railway Preservation Society. (Phil Tatt/Online Transport Archive)

STORES CARS

The first dedicated stores cars acquired by the LCC were two – Nos 05 and 06 – that entered service in 1905. Designated Class J, the two cars were fitted with Brill 21E four-wheel trucks. Smaller than the later Class K cars, both were to pass to the ownership of the LPTB in July 1933. Here, No 05 is seen at Penhall Road on 28 May 1950; this was during the period when the future 'Tramatorium' was under construction (work commenced in January 1950 and would be completed in the late summer). (John Meredith/Online Transport Archive)

Alongside the ex-Poole & District tram converted into a railgrinder in 1921 – a vehicle sold to the Llandudno & Colwyn Bay Electric Railway in 1936 – Bournemouth Corporation also operated a single dedicated stores van. This was No B, which was supplied in 1903 by G.F. Milnes & Co, a company that had constructed the fleet's first fifty-four passenger cars, on a Peckham Cantilever four-wheel truck.
(D.W.K. Jones Collection/Online Transport Archive)

During 1906 and 1907, Milnes Voss of Birkenhead supplied six works cars – Nos 1-6 – to Birmingham Corporation on M&G-built 21E trucks. Although Nos 1-5 were initially built as salt cars, they were to operate as stores cars whilst No 6 – delivered in 1907 – operated as a stores car from new. It was fitted with a hoist and job for the lifting of heavy loads. Of the six, only Nos 4 and 6 were operational post-1913, being supplemented by a second No 5, constructed in the corporation's Kyotts Lake Road that year. No 4 was subsequently to be converted into a tower wagon – see page 54 – but No 6 was used after 1913 initially as a ticket audit office at Hockley depot. It had a varied career thereafter until December 1939, when it was withdrawn following the closure of Hockley depot. Although out of use, it was to survive through the war, not being sold for scrap until mid-1945.
(D.W.K. Jones Collection/Online Transport Archive)

In 1908, the LCC constructed four larger store vans – Nos 07–10 – that were equipped with M&G four-wheel trucks. All four, which were designated Class K by the LCC, were to pass to LPTB ownership in July 1933 and No 09, now in LPTB ownership, is pictured here at West Croydon station. It was to survive in service until May 1949. (Barry Cross Collection/Online Transport Archive)

The LCC discovered that, whilst usual stores vans could accommodate most items, there was a need for vehicles that could accommodate heavier loads. As a result, two Class L open wagons were acquired in 1909. Constructed on M&G radial trucks, Nos 011 and 012 were designated by the LCC as wheel carriers. Both were to survive to be taken over by the LPTB in July 1933 and were to be withdrawn for scrap during the final elimination of London's trams between 1950 and 1952. Here, No 011 is pictured outside Charlton Works. (R.W.A. Jones/Online Transport Archive)

The first electric trams operated by Liverpool Corporation were fifteen power car and trailers supplied by the German company W.C.F. Busch of Eimsbuttel, Hamburg, in 1898. Numbered 400-29 – with even numbers being the power cars, odd numbers being trailers – the trams were fitted with four-wheel trucks supplied by another German company, Schuckhert. Destined to have a short life – they were offered for sale in 1901 although there were no buyers and they remained in stock until the First World War when the majority were scrapped – a number were converted into works cars; one so treated was trailer No 429 which was to become a tools van at Garston in 1914. As such, it survived for more than 30 years; it was only in July 1950 that the tram was moved – by rail – for disposal at Edge Lane works, where it was recorded. Acquired for preservation along with 'Bellamy' car No 558, No 429 was stored in the open at Kirkby where vandalism took its toll and both were subsequently scrapped. (Phil Tatt/Online Transport Archive)

During the 1920s and 1930s Leeds Corporation undertook the replacement of a number of older works cars. Amongst those converted as new works cars was No 198 which became stores van No 5 in July 1927. The tram was one of a batch of 100 trams supplied by ERTCW during 1901 and 1902 on Brill 21E four-wheel trucks. Originally open-top, No 198 received a top cover in 1908 but only gained its enclosed lower-deck vestibules after conversion into a works car. In 1951, Leeds Corporation renumbered stores car No 5 as 8A and it is pictured here, with two match wagons on Beeston Road, after this renumbering. The car was to be fitted with enclosed vestibules in January 1954. The Beeston route was converted to bus operation on 19 November 1955. No 8A was to survive for longer, not being withdrawn until the final demise of the tramway system in November 1959. (Phil Tatt/Online Transport Archive)

Another conversion undertaken by Leeds Corporation was No 73A, which emerged as new stores car No 2 in 1937, this car had originally been supplied by Brush in 1904 as one of a batch of 25 trams that were the first open-balcony top-covered trams supplied to the corporation. Initially number 73, it acquired lower-deck vestibules in 1912 and was to become No 73A in 1926 when a new generation of Brush-built cars entered service. Here, No 2 is seen here on Boar Lane viewed towards City Square with the old Norwich Union Building, which was demolished and replaced in the 1960s. (F.E.J. Ward/Online Transport Archive)

The previous year (1936), Leeds undertook the conversion of a further tram into a stores car. No 248A – which had originally been No 248 when new in 1901 (when it was delivered as an open-top car by ERTCW on a Brill 21E four-wheel truck; it received a top cover in 1907 and enclosed lower-deck vestibules six years later) – emerged as No. 3, becoming No. 4A in April 1951, and is seen here in the corporation's PW yard at Sovereign Street in the early 1950s. It was fitted with a 1,000 gallon water tank in early 1953 and was finally scrapped in December 1959. (Phil Tatt/Online Transport Archive)

With the decline of the Hull Corporation network, culminating in the system's final closure in 1945, Leeds Corporation purchased a number of passenger cars in 1942 and 1945. In addition to these, Leeds also acquired Hull No 96, which had been used on Humberside as a stores car and snow plough since conversion in 1933. No 96 had originally been constructed by Hurst Nelson, one of a batch of 10 (Nos 91-100) open-top cars on Brill 21E trucks and had been fully enclosed in 1930. Numbered 6 in the Leeds Corporation works fleet and used as a stores car, the tram – seen here at Roundhay – was to survive through until the final closure of the Leeds system in November 1959. Acquired locally for preservation, the tram was initially stored on the Middleton Railway, where it avoided the fate of other trams stored there (scrapped after vandalism), and then Wakefield and again Leeds, before it was acquired by the Manchester Tramway Museum Society for use on the Heaton Park tramway. Now restored as a single-deck passenger car, as Hull No 96, the tram has been operational since 1988. (Phil Tatt/Online Transport Archive)

Dublin United Tramways stores car No 73 was the third works car in the city to carry this fleet number; originally passenger car No 1 – one of the first batch of electric cars supplied by G.F. Milnes & Co in 1896 and supplied to the Dublin Southern District Tramways – and fitted with a Peckham truck, the tram was converted for works duties during the 1930s. It was one of the handful of DUT works cars to survive through until towards the end of the system and is pictured here after the take-over of the DUT system by CIÉ. Alongside No 73 is water car (lorry) No 4 – see water car No 1 on page 118 – which was fitted with a Brill truck and which was also to survive until towards the end. Withdrawn in 1949, the body and tank were to survive for some years in use on a farm in County Louth. (F.N.T. Lloyd-Jones/Online Transport Archive)

Sheffield Corporation No 349, pictured here at Tinsley depot, was the only stores van to survive until the final closure of the system in October 1960. The tram had originally been UEC-built double-deck car No 271. This was one of 15 open balcony trams supplied by the company in 1907; originally fitted with M&G radial trucks, all were to receive Peckham P22 trucks between 1918 and 1920. The tram was renumbered 349 in 1937 and was converted for works duties in January 1951 – the penultimate car to be so treated by the corporation. Fitted with illuminations, No 349 was to feature in the procession that marked the closure of the Sheffield system and was acquired by the Tramway Museum Society, being used as a mobile generator at Crich until September 1967, when it was up for spares. The four-wheel truck was used in the restoration of Chesterfield No 7. (Phil Tatt/Online Transport Archive)

The last 'new' works car to be converted by Birmingham Corporation was No 341; this was one of a batch of 60 balcony top cars, Nos 301-60, supplied by UEC in 1911. In 1945, No 341 was modified to act as the illuminated car celebrating victory in the Second World War. In January 1948, the tram was converted into a single-deck supply car, being allocated for the purpose to Selly Oak depot. As a result of the conversion, No 341 was the last of the type to survive in service, not being withdrawn until July 1952 and the final closure of Selly Oak depot. Although there was possible interest from the Llandudno & Colwyn Bay Electric Railway in its purchase, this was too late as work on scrapping the car at Witton depot had already commenced. (F.N.T. Lloyd-Jones/Online Transport Archive)

WATER CARS

Leeds Corporation, having acquired two horse-drawn water carts during 1897, was to acquire an electric-powered example the following year. The 2,000-gallon tank was supplied by Greenwood & Batley Ltd at a cost of £500. The car was fitted with a Peckham Cantilever 8A four-wheel truck. Its fate is unknown but was probably withdrawn around the start of the First World War. (D.W.K. Jones Collection/Online Transport Archive)

A busy view of Patrick Street in Cork sees no fewer than four of the passenger cars of the 900mm-gauge Cork Electric Tramways & Lighting Co Ltd with, in the centre, the fleet's water car. The company had two dedicated works cars – the water car illustrated here and a permanent way car, both of which were constructed at the company's Albert Road depot – and a horse-drawn tower wagon. The Cork system, which extended over almost 10 route miles, survived from 22 December 1898 through to 30 September 1931. (Barry Cross Collection/Online Transport Archive)

Dublin United Tramways operated a number of water cars – or lorries as they were known locally – the first of which, No 1 (illustrated here with a four-wheel wagon possibly in Clontarf depot), dated to 1899. Nos 2 and 3 were similar whilst No 4 had a full-length canopy. (Barry Cross Collection/Online Transport Archive)

Pictured in Donnybrook depot is DUT water car No 4; its construction date is uncertain. Fitted with a Brill four-wheel truck, this was the only one of the four water cars to survive the Second World War and, following withdrawal in 1949, the vehicle was used for some years as a static water tank at Mellifont Abbey in County Louth. (Barry Cross Collection/Online Transport Archive)

For the opening of the City of Hull Tramways in July 1899, the corporation acquired some thirty open-top four-wheel passenger trams and two dedicated water cars; the latter were constructed in the USA by J.G. Brill Co of Philadelphia and were fitted with the same manufacturer's 21E four-wheel truck. One of the duo, No 2, is recorded here behind Holderness Road depot. (W.A. Camwell/National Tramway Museum)

The provenance of Dover Corporation's unnumbered water car is uncertain – it was possibly the work of Dick, Kerr & Co of Kilmarnock and possibly utilised a Brill 21E four-wheel truck – although the records suggest that it was ordered in April 1900. Prior to its construction, the corporation had used a passenger car for its works duties. The tram was to survive after the First World War – albeit little used after the war – and seems to have been disposed of by 1927. (Barry Cross Collection/Online Transport Archive)

Shortly after the opening of the Nottingham Corporation system in 1901, ERTCW supplied two dedicated works cars. No 1, seen here, was a water car whilst No 2 was a snow plough. Both were fitted with Brill 21E trucks. (Harry Luff Collection/Online Transport Archive)

The majority of Sheffield Corporation's works cars were converted from redundant passenger stock; however, there were two purpose-built water cars; No 130 that was new in 1901 and No 212, completed three years later. The former is pictured here when new; it was converted to act as a snow clearer in 1905 and was to be withdrawn in 1921. No 212 was to last longer; renumbered 372 in 1935, the car was finally to be withdrawn in December 1950. (Barry Cross Collection/Online Transport Archive)

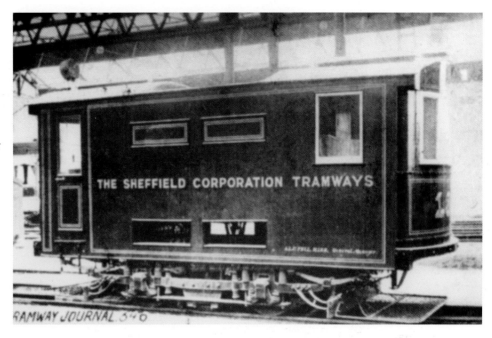

Between 1901 and 1903, the LUT acquired three water cars – Nos 1-3 (later 001-003) – that were fitted with Brill 21E four-wheel trucks. No 002, illustrated here alongside MET breakdown car No 7, was new in 1902; it was to be scrapped in 1931. The other two – Nos 001 and 003 – passed to the LPTB in 1933 but were destined to have a relatively short life in new ownership, being scrapped in 1938 and 1935 respectively. MET No 07 was new in 1922; becoming part of the LPTB as well, it was scrapped in 1938. (Barry Cross Collection/Online Transport Archive)

Wolverhampton Corporation No A1, seen here when new around 1902, was a combined water car and snow plough. Constructed by ERTCW and fitted with a Brill 21E four-wheel truck, No A1 was to be rebuilt by M&G in 1908 at the same time as this manufacturer supplied a second combined water car and snow plough – No A3. The third dedicated works car built for the corporation was a salt trailer constructed by G.F. Milnes & Co and delivered in about 1904. (Barry Cross Collection/Online Transport Archive)

The only purpose-built works car acquired by Stockport Corporation was No 100; this was a water car built by Dick, Kerr & Co Ltd of Preston on a Brill 21E four-wheel truck in 1902. (Geoffrey Morant Collection/Online Transport Archive)

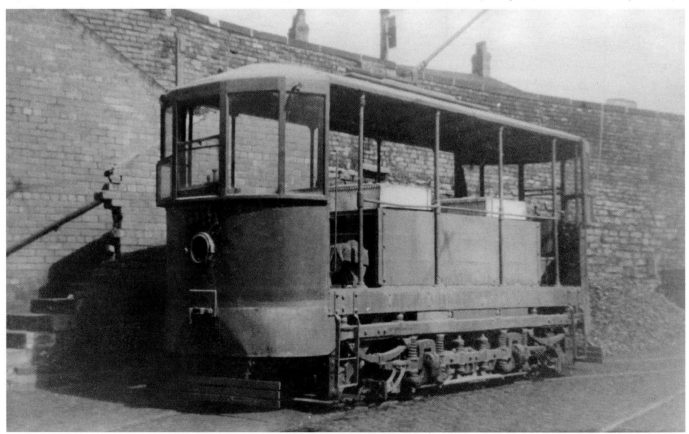

Initially, the South Lancashire Tramways Co possessed a single dedicated works car; this was water car No 1 that was new in August 1902. Built by the British Electric Car Co Ltd on the same manufacturer's SB40 four-wheel truck, the car was latterly used as a snow plough and was scrapped by 1931. A second works car was acquired from the Middleton Electric Traction Co Ltd in October 1925 when that operator was acquired by Manchester Corporation. In addition, three redundant passenger cars were converted into snow ploughs between 1921 and 1927. (Barry Cross Collection/Online Transport Archive)

In 1902, Cardiff Corporation took delivery of its sole dedicated works car, a combined water car and sweeper that was built by ERTCW on a Brill 21E four-wheel truck. Unnumbered when new, the tram was to become No 131 in 1905; this number was carried until 1926, when it was again to operate without a number. It was fitted with a 1,000-gallon tank and was initially open; the body was enclosed by 1913. It is pictured here on Heathfield Road on 2 December 1945 in the unlined grey livery in which it operated from 1916; prior to that date, it had been painted in a crimson lake and white livery. Preserved on withdrawal in 1950 (the only ex-Cardiff electric tram to survive), the car was restored to its 1913 livery prior to departing its home city. It is now part of the National Tramway Museum collection. (Ian L. Wright/Online Transport Archive)

The standard gauge system operated by Ayr Corporation between 1901 and 1931 operated a single car specifically designed for works duties; this was water car No 17, pictured here when new in 1903, built by Hurst Nelson on a Brill 21E four-wheel truck. The water tank could accommodate 2,340 gallons. (Barry Cross Collection/Online Transport Archive)

Ilford Corporation's sole dedicated works car was a water car, No 1, that was supplied by BEC on Brill 22E bogies in 1903. Fitted with a 1,800-gallon tank, No 1 survived through to the creation of the LPTB in July 1933 and was renumbered 057 by its new owners. However, the tram was not to survive long thereafter; it was withdrawn and scrapped in 1937 as a result of the conversion of the east London tram routes to trolleybus operation. (Barry Cross Collection/Online Transport Archive)

The first dedicated works car acquired by the MET was a water car – No 1 – that was built by the company and fitted with a Brush A truck. New in 1904, the vehicle was to survive in service until being withdrawn in 1931. (D.W.K. Jones Collection/ Online Transport Archive)

The first of Leicester Corporation's fleet of water cars – No 100 – is pictured when new. The tram was supplied by ERTCW on a Brill 21E truck in 1904. Two further water cars were operated by the corporation; Nos 142 and 143 were supplied by UEC in 1909 and 1913 respectively and were also fitted with Brill 21E trucks. All three were fitted with 1,800-gallon tanks and could operate as railgrinders as well. The trio became Nos 151-53 in 1912 and Nos 179-81 in 1920 as the corporation passenger fleet continued to grow. No 181 was subsequently fitted with a tower. (Barry Cross Collection/ Online Transport Archive)

Belfast Corporation acquired two water cars – Nos A and B – in 1905 and 1906 respectively; they were built by M&G. Pictured here is No A; this was to survive in service until 1932 whilst No B was to survive for a further decade, not being withdrawn until 1942. (Barry Cross Collection/Online Transport Archive)

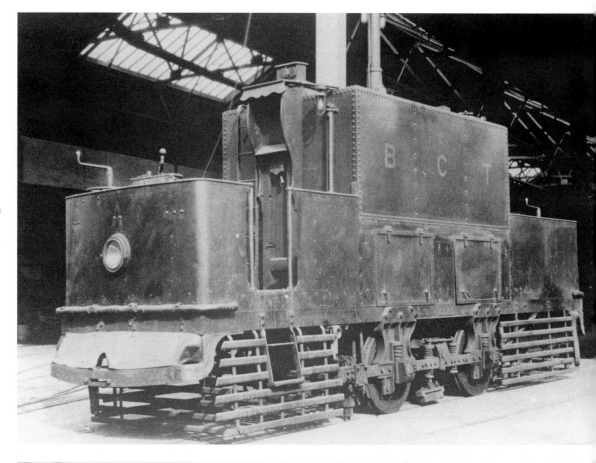

In 1905, Leith Corporation acquired a single works car; this was a watercar – No 60 – that was built by UEC on a Brill 21E four-wheel truck. On 2 November 1920, ownership and operation of the Leith tramway passed to Edinburgh Corporation. This included No 60, which was to be renumbered as No 1 in the Edinburgh works fleet and it is in this guise that the tram was recorded here. (Barry Cross Collection/ Online Transport Archive)

CORPORATION TRAMWAYS

As with a number of other systems, the tramways operated by the Walthamstow UDC (later Corporation) Light Railways employed a sole dedicated works tram – an unnumbered railgrinder – that was new in 1905. Built by Brush on the same company's Type A four-wheel truck. This view records the car whilst still in Walthamstow ownership; it passed to the LPTB in July 1933, being renumbered 63K, although it was not to survive long in new ownership, being withdrawn for scrap later the same year. (Robin Barratt Collection/Online Transport Archive)

West Ham Corporation acquired two water cars; although unnumbered when new, they were eventually to become Nos 1A (new in 1905) and 2A (new in 1906). The larger of the two, with a 2,000-gallon water tank, was the former, which is pictured when new; this also acted as a sweeper. Both of the cars were supplied by M&G and were fitted with that manufacturer's four-wheel truck. Although No 2A was to be withdrawn before the LPTB took over in 1933, No 1A did pass to the new owners but was not to last long, being withdrawn later the same year. (Barry Cross Collection/Online Transport Archive)

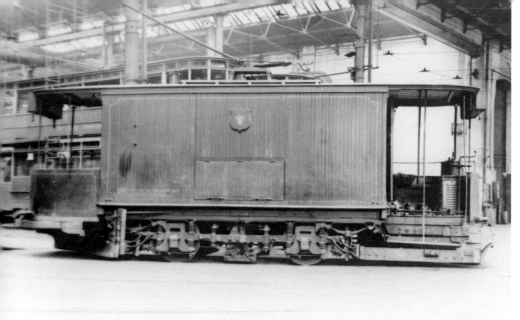

Alongside its fleet of sixty passenger cars, Bury Corporation operated a single works car; this was an unnumbered water car cum railgrinder that was supplied in 1906 by Mountain & Gibson fitted with that company's own 21EM four-wheel truck. This side view, taken in the corporation's sole depot on Rochdale Road, shows that the vehicle was also fitted with snow ploughs. In addition to this vehicle, Bury Corporation also owned three unpowered salt wagons; these were supplied by BEC and new in 1904. (Barry Cross Collection/Online Transport Archive)

Glasgow Corporation No 16, pictured here in the yard at Barrland Street, dated originally to 1907. No 6 when first constructed, the tram was fitted with vestibuled ends in 1935 and further modified in 1953. As No 16, the car was to survive through until the final closure of the system in September 1962. Glasgow's works trams were painted either in crimson lake – as seen here – or dark brown; until the 1930s, the livery was relieved with lining out. Latterly, even the fleet name was often omitted. (Ian Stewart/Online Transport Archive)

In July 1907, Glasgow Corporation took delivery of two further water cars; fitted with Brill 21E trucks, these were originally numbered 8 and 9 but were eventually renumbered 18 and 19 respectively. The latter is seen at the PW yard at Barrland Street on 13 June 1962. The two cars were originally unvestibuled but received enclosed platforms in May 1928 (No 18) and August 1936 (No 19). As can be seen in the photograph, No 19 had no access to the nearside front cab. No 18, which spent some time as an illuminated car during the 1930s, was withdrawn in April but No 19, which also acted as a track scrubber, was to survive until the system's closure. Les Collings/Online Transport Archive

Chesterfield Corporation possessed a sole dedicated works car; this was No 15, a water car that was completed in 1909. The car, which was fitted with a 2,000-gallon water tank, was constructed by Brush and used a Brush Special Flexible four-wheel truck. The tram is seen here in the corporation's depot at Chatsworth Road. (Barry Cross Collection/Online Transport Archive)

Shortly before the First World War – the exact date is uncertain as both 1907 and 1912 have been cited – Croydon Corporation acquired a replacement water car. This was supplied by UEC on a Brill 21E truck and was fitted with a 1,500-gallon water tank. It was not to operate as a water car for long; after having been used as part of a recruitment campaign in late 1914, following the outbreak of war, the tram was converted into a welding car during 1916. During this work, the tram lost its water tank in place of a wooden body with a sliding door. Access to the trolleypole was achieved by means of a ladder and handrail affixed to one side. It is in this guise that the tram was recorded whilst still in corporation ownership; surviving to be taken over by the LPTB in July 1933, the tram, renumbered 056, was transferred to West Ham depot. It was eventually to be scrapped at Walthamstow depot; again, the date is uncertain as both October 1936 and post-December 1937 have been cited. (Barry Cross Collection/Online Transport Archive)

LPTB No 056 is pictured towards the end of its life as it awaits scrapping at Walthamstow depot. (Barry Cross Collection/ Online Transport Archive)

Rochdale Corporation's unnumbered water car demonstrates its effectiveness on the Esplanade in front of the Town Hall. Built by Brush in 1912, probably on the same manufacturer's AA four-wheel truck, the water car was Rochdale's sole purpose-built works car. Apart from its prime duty – it had been part-funded by the corporation's cleansing department – the vehicle also carried railgrinding and welding equipment whilst it could also act as a snow plough if required. An unpowered trailer was acquired by the cleansing department in 1916 to act as a sand spreader; this was towed when required by the water car. (J. Joyce Collection/Online Transport Archive)

South Shields Corporation possessed three works cars; one was a water car that was originally supplied by Brush, on a Brush flexible four-wheel truck, in 1913. Originally unnumbered, the car was to become No 11 in 1930. Although primarily a water car, as evinced in this view, taken before it became No 11, the tram was pressed into other duties, on this occasion acting as a snow plough. The tram was fitted with a 2,000-gallon tank with the water being sprayed initially by an electric pump and, later in its career, by pressure. A siding was located at the Market Place where a pump was installed for refilling the tank when necessary. (Barry Cross Collection/Online Transport Archive)

Coventry Corporation water car No 10 – pictured here outside Priestley's Bridge depot – had an interesting career that spanned both the steam and electric eras. Built originally as a steam trailer – No 5 of 1884 by Brush – the tram was converted into an uncanopied open-top electric car in 1895, when it was fitted with a Peckham Cantilever truck. Although sister cars Nos 6-8 were further rebuilt in 1904/05, No 5 was not so treated and was initially withdrawn in 1915 after suffering fire damage. Its truck and underframe were then utilised for the construction of a new hopper vehicle – No 5 – in 1920, before undergoing a further conversion into a water car – as No 10 – in the late 1920s. (Barry Cross Collection/Online Transport Archive)

Operation of the conduit system in London – as Blackpool had experienced in 1885 when introducing electric trams to England – brought a range of problems that did not affect tramways powered by the more usual overhead. One of these was the accumulation of material in the conduit itself; in order to ensure the smooth operation of the system, the conduit had to be cleaned out on a regular basis and, in 1925, the LCC acquired a Yorkshire seven-ton service vehicle, registered XX781, that operated as a conduit steam cleaning van. Numbered originally 18 and latterly as No 159, it was allocated in later years to the Department of the Chief Engineer (Permanent Way Engineer) and based at Walthamstow depot. Withdrawn from there in early 1948, it was sold in November that year. (J. Joyce Collection/Online Transport Archive)

In 1929, the LCC acquired this six-ton tramway breakdown tender with crane from Karrier Motors Ltd of Huddersfield. Number 89 by the LCC and registered UW1264, it was to become No 173K in the LPTB service fleet and is seen here on 2 April 1951 assisting 'E/1' class No 1391 in towing another 'E/1' – No 1493 – out of Addington Street. At this date, the vehicle was based at Vauxhall; two months later it was transferred to Holloway. Following brief spells at Muswell Hill and Walworth, No 173K was finally withdrawn for good in May 1952 and was sold off three months later. (John Meredith/Online Transport Archive)

Pictured at Thornton Heath in November 1944 is London Transport tower wagon 5E (HX386) that had originally been supplied to the MET in June 1930 (fleet No 118). This Associated Daimler 418 six-ton vehicle was fitted with solid tyres until pneumatic tyres were first fitted in September 1940 and was to be withdrawn in September 1948. Following withdrawal, its tower was transferred to No 728J whilst the remainder was sold for scrap in June 1949. (Geoffrey Ashwell/Online Transport Archive)

Between June 1935 and October 1936, the LPTB acquired sixteen AEC Mercury four-ton tower wagons – Nos 75Q to 90Q. No 79Q (BYM148), pictured here, was one of the earlier examples, being new in July 1935 and originally numbered 154. These vehicles were used for both the tram and trolleybus networks and, post-war, No 79Q spent time allocated to both Bexleyheath garage and Bowles Road PW depot. By the late 1950s, with the conversion of the trolleybus routes to bus operation, the requirement for tower wagons was much reduced and No 79Q was withdrawn from service on 1 January 1960; it was sold in April the same year. (Phil Tatt/Online Transport Archive)

In January 1937, Dundee Corporation acquired a batch of fifteen single-deck Daimler COG5 buses fitted with Cowieson 36-seat bodies, Nos 7-21. YJ4113 was originally numbered 20, becoming No 7 in 1942 and No A7 five years later. Seven of the batch were transferred to the War Department in 1940. No 20 was withdrawn in 1951 and was one of two of the type to be converted after withdrawal into a tower wagon; it became No 2 whilst YJ4104 (ex-No 11), one of the batch passed to the War Department in 1940, was to become No 1. No 1 was to be scrapped after the withdrawal of the final trams in October 1956, whilst No 2 was to survive a further decade in corporation use, not being sold for scrap until 1968. (Phil Tatt/Online Transport Archive)

In January 1942, the LPTB acquired a Fordson 24hp tractor from the Ford Motor Co Ltd of Dagenham. No 627X was transferred to Charlton Works in February 1949 where it and similar No 629X were employed as shunters in the yard at Penhall Road – where No 627X is seen in this view – moving trams and other vehicles as the process of scrapping London's trams progressed. No 627X was to remain allocated to Charlton for this work until August 1953 when it was transferred to Aldenham Works. It was finally to be sold in November 1955. (Phil Tatt/Online Transport Archive)

Delivered new to Liverpool Corporation in 1946, this Guy Vixen tower wagon No 51 GKD317 is pictured alongside 'Baby Grand' No 263. The Guy was used for tramway work through to the end of the system in September 1957 and was then utilised by the corporation for streetlighting work until finally withdrawn in the late 1970s. Preserved on withdrawal, the vehicle is now part of the Wirral Transport Museum collection where, in connection with the Birkenhead tramway, it has now regained its original tram-related role.
(W.G.S. Hyde/Online Transport Archive)

Over the years, Blackpool Corporation has operated a number of tower wagons. In 1948, Karrier supplied two, Nos 238/239, that were fitted with hydraulic platforms supplied by Eagle Engineering Ltd of Warwick. No 238 (CFV925) is seen inside Rigby Road depot. This vehicle was to survive in service until 1965; No 239 was to survive a further three years. (F.E.J. Ward/ Online Transport Archive)

London Transport was one of many operators who reused redundant buses as the basis of works road vehicles. Pictured in the traverser at Penhall Road is 720J (GK5344), which was a towing lorry based at Plumstead. This had originally been ST523 – one of 1,138 double-deckers delivered between 1929 and 1932 – and re-entered service in this form during February 1948. It was to remain active until final withdrawal in June 1955. (Phil Tatt/Online Transport Archive)

Tower wagon 728J (AXM662) was another redundant bus converted by London Transport and was rebuilt from STL401, entering service in its new role in December 1948. It was to outlast London's trams, falling victim once the programme of trolleybus to bus conversion commenced in the late 1950s. It was sold for scrap to George Cohen in April 1959. (Julian Thompson/Online Transport Archive)

Another conversion by London Transport from a withdrawn double-deck bus was tower wagon No 729J (AGX529) had that originally been No STL190; the bus was converted into a tower wagon in April 1949 with work involving the transfer of the tower from an earlier wagon (No 6E). When new, the wagon was allocated to Rye Lane Permanent Way depot. The wagon was to survive in service through to the early stages of the trolleybus conversion programme, being sold in July 1959. (Phil Tatt/Online Transport Archive)

BIBLIOGRAPHY

ANDERSON, R.C., *The Tramways of East Anglia*, LRTL; 1969

BADDELEY, G.E., ed, *The Tramways of Kent – Volume 1*; 'Invicta', LRTL and TLRS; 1971

BADDELEY, G.E., ed, *The Tramways of Kent – Volume 2*; 'Invicta', LRTL and TLRS; 1975

BADDELEY, G.E., edited by PRICE, J.H., *The Tramways of Kent*, LRTA; undated

BETT, W.H. and GILHAM, J.C., edited by PRICE, J.H., *The Tramways of North Lancashire*, LRTA; undated

BETT, W.H. and GILHAM, J.C., edited by PRICE, J.H., *The Tramways of North-East England*, LRTL; undated

BETT, W.H. and GILHAM, J.C., edited by PRICE, J.H., *The Tramways of South Wales*, LRTA; undated

BETT, W.H. and GILHAM, J.C., edited by PRICE, J.H., *The Tramways of South-West England*, LRTA; undated

BETT, W.H. and GILHAM, J.C., edited by PRICE, J.H., *The Tramways of South-East Lancashire*, LRTL; undated

BETT, W.H. and GILHAM, J.C., edited by PRICE, J.H., *The Tramways of the East Midlands*, LRTL; undated

BETT, W.H. and GILHAM, J.C., edited by PRICE, J.H., *The Tramways of the East Midlands*, LRTL; undated

BETT, W.H. and GILHAM, J.C., edited by PRICE, J.H., *The Tramways of the South Midlands*, LRTA; undated

BETT, W.H. and GILHAM, J.C., edited by PRICE, J.H., *The Tramways of Yorkshire and Humberside*, LRTA; undated

BETT, W.H. and GILHAM, J.C., edited by WISEMAN, R.J.S., *The Tramways of the West Midlands*, LRTA; undated

BROOK, Roy, *Huddersfield Corporation Tramways*, Author; 1983

BROTCHIE, Alan W., *Scottish Tramway Fleets*, N. B. Traction; 1968

BURROWS, V.E., *The Tramways of Southend-on-Sea*, Advertiser Press; 1965

CORCORAN, Michael, *Through Streets Broad and Narrow*, Midland Publishing; 2000

GANDY, Kenneth, *Sheffield Corporation Tramways*, Sheffield City Libraries; 1985

GILHAM, J.C. and WISEMAN, R.J.S., *The Tramways of the South Coast*, LRTA; undated

GILHAM, J.C. and WISEMAN, R.J.S., *The Tramways of West Yorkshire*, LRTA; undated

GILHAM, J.C. and WISEMAN, R.J.S., *The Tramways of Western Scotland*, LRTA; undated

GILLHAM, J.C. and WISEMAN, R.J.S., *The Tramways of Eastern Scotland*, LRTA; undated

GILLHAM, J.C. and WISEMAN, R.J.S., *The Tramways of South Lancashire and North Wales*, LRTA; undated

HARLEY, Robert J., *Croydon Tramways: A history of trams in the Croydon area from 1879 to 1951*, Capital Transport; 2004

HEARSE, George S., *The Tramways of Jarrow and South Shields*, Author; 1971

HEARSE, George S., *The Tramways of Northumberland*, Author; 1961

HORNE, J.B. and MAUND, T.B., *Liverpool Transport: Volume 1 – 1830-1900*, LRTL; 1975

HORNE, J.B. and MAUND, T.B., *Liverpool Transport: Volume 4 – 1939-1957*, TPC; 1989

JORDAN, H.E., *The Tramways of Reading*, LRTL; 1957

KING, J.S., *Bradford Corporation Tramways*, Venture Publications; 1999

LAWSON, P.W., *Birmingham Corporation Tramway Rolling Stock,* Birmingham Transport Historical Group; 1963

MAUND, T.B. and JENKINS, M., *The Tramways of Birkenhead and Wallasey,* LRTA; 1987

MAYBIN, J.M., *Belfast Corporation Tramways,* LRTA; undated

OAKLEY, E.R., *London County Council Tramways – Volume 2: North London,* London Transport History Group; 1991

OAKLEY, E.R. and HOLLAND, C.E., *London Transport Tramways 1933-1952,* London Tramways Historical Group; 1998

PROUDLOCK, Noel, *Leeds: A History of its Tramways,* Author; 1991

SAMBOURNE, R.C., *Plymouth: 100 Years of Street Travel,* R. C. Sambourne; Glasney Press; undated

SMEETON, C.S., *The London United Tramways: Volume 2 – 1913-1913,* LRTA; 2000

SMEETON, C.S., *The Metropolitan Electric Tramways: Vol 2 – 1921-33,* LRTL/TLRS; 1986

SOPER, J., *Leeds Transport: Volume 2 – 1902-1931,* Leeds Transport Historical Society; 1996

SOPER, J., *Leeds Transport: Volume 3 – 1903-1953,* Leeds Transport Historical Society; 2003

SOPER, J., *Leeds Transport: Volume 4 – 1953-1974,* Leeds Transport Historical Society; 2007

STADDON, S.A., *The Tramways of Sunderland,* Advertiser Press; 1974

STEWART, Ian, *The Glasgow Tramcar,* Scottish Tramway Museum Society; 1983

The Tramways of Croydon, 'Southmet'; LRTL; 1960

The Tramways of East London, 'Rodinglea'; TLRS and LRTL; 1967

THORNTON, Eric and KING, Stanley, *Halifax Corporation Tramways,* LRTA; 2004

TURNER, Keith, SMITH, Shirley and SMITH, Paul, *The Directory of British Tram Depots,* OPC; 2001

TURNER, Keith, *The Llandudno & Colwyn Bay Electric Railway,* Oakwood Press; 1993

VOICE, David, *Works Tramcars of the British Isles,* Adam Gordon; 2008

WALLER, Peter, *Regional Tramways: Scotland,* Pen & Sword; 2016

WALLER, Peter, *Regional Tramways: The North-West England post-1945,* Pen & Sword; 2017

WALLER, Peter, *Regional Tramways: Wales, Isle of Man & Ireland post-1945,* Pen & Sword; 2017

WALLER, Peter, *Regional Tramways: Midlands & Southern England,* Pen & Sword; 2018

WALLER, Peter, *Regional Tramways: Yorkshire & North-East of England,* Pen & Sword; 2016

WAYWELL, Robin and JUX, Frank, *Industrial Railways & Locomotives of the County of London,* Industrial Railway Society; 2008

WEBB, J.S., *Black Country Tramways: Volume 1 – 1872-1912,* Author; 1974

WEBB, J.S., *Black Country Tramways: Volume 2 including Kidderminster & Stourport Tramways,* Author; 1976

YEARSLEY, Ian and GROVES, Philip, *The Manchester Tramways,* TPC; 1988

YOUNG, Tony, *Tramways in Rochdale: Steam, Electric and Metrolink,* LRTA; 2008